HUMANE
REPRODUCTION

HUMANE
REPRODUCTION

*Formulated by the Committee on
Preventive Psychiatry*

GROUP FOR THE ADVANCEMENT OF PSYCHIATRY,

CHARLES SCRIBNER'S SONS · NEW YORK

1 3 5 7 9 11 13 15 17 19 C/C 20 18 16 14 12 10 8 6 4 2
1 3 5 7 9 11 13 15 17 19 C/P 20 18 16 14 12 10 8 6 4 2

Printed in the United States of America
Library of Congress Catalog Card Number 73-11574
ISBN 0-684-13639-2 (cloth)
ISBN 0-684-13641-4 (paper)

It cannot be denied that Malthusian concerns become a necessity in married life at some time or other. Theoretically it would be one of the greatest triumphs of mankind, one of the most compassionate liberations from natural bondage to which we are subject, were it possible to raise the responsible act of procreation to a level of voluntary and intentional behavior, and to free this act from its entanglement with our indispensable satisfaction of a natural desire.

SIGMUND FREUD
"Sexuality in the Etiology of the Neuroses"

STATEMENT OF PURPOSE

The Group for the Advancement of Psychiatry has a membership of approximately 300 psychiatrists, most of whom are organized in the form of a number of working committees. These committees direct their efforts toward the study of various aspects of psychiatry and the application of this knowledge to the fields of mental health and human relations.

Collaboration with specialists in other disciplines has been and is one of GAP's working principles. Since the formation of GAP in 1946 its members have worked closely with such other specialists as anthropologists, biologists, economists, statisticians, educators, lawyers, nurses, psychologists, sociologists, social workers, and experts in mass communication, philosophy, and semantics. GAP envisages a continuing program of work according to the following aims:

(1) To collect and appraise significant data in the field of psychiatry, mental health, and human relations;

(2) To re-evaluate old concepts and to develop and test new ones;

(3) To apply the knowledge thus obtained for the promotion of mental health and good human relations.

GAP is an independent group, and its reports represent the composite findings and opinions of its members only, guided by its many consultants.

Humane Reproduction was formulated by the Committee on Preventive Psychiatry. Its members are listed at the end of the Acknowledgments, in which the assistance of GAP contributing members and Fellows and of other consultants is recognized. Members of all committees of GAP are listed at the end of the book.

ACKNOWLEDGMENTS

For assistance in the preparation of this book the Committee on Preventive Psychiatry is grateful to the following contributing members of GAP: Gerald Caplan, Jules V. Coleman, Leonard J. Duhl, Albert J. Glass, Harold M. Visotsky, and Stanley F. Yolles; and to the following GAP Fellows: H. Lane Ferree, Scott Nelson, and Steven S. Sharfstein. Among the consultants who also aided the committee, Viola W. Bernard is a member of GAP's Committee on Social Issues; the others, who are not members of GAP, are: John B. Calhoun, James P. Comer, Angelo D'Agostino, S.J., Lincoln H. Day, Mark Flapan, Adele Morrison, Mark Perlman, Alice Rossi, Helene Schoenfeld, and Christopher Tietze. In the preparation of the index Dr. Calhoun was assisted by Anne E. Hardman. Professor Rossi also provided a critical review of the manuscript, and Mrs. Louise H. Fleck and Mrs. Catherine Molloy furnished valuable editorial help.

COMMITTEE ON PREVENTIVE PSYCHIATRY
GROUP FOR THE ADVANCEMENT OF PSYCHIATRY

Stephen Fleck, M.D., *Chairman*
Frederick Gottlieb, M.D.
Benjamin Jeffries, M.D.
Ruth W. Lidz, M.D.
E. James Lieberman, M.D.
Mary E. Mercer, M.D.
Harris V. Peck, M.D.
Marvin E. Perkins, M.D.

CONTENTS

HUMANE
REPRODUCTION

one | INTRODUCTION

For thousands of years, the news of pregnancy and its culmination in the birth of a child have usually been a cause for
joy and celebration. At the same time, both the birth itself
and the care of the mother and child afterwards have also
been the source of great and realistic anxieties, because survival of either mother or child was far from assured. During
the past hundred years, medical advances have helped minimize the risks. In the past, a large number of children in a
family was usually considered desirable, especially in agricultural societies. Nevertheless, some nomadic societies have
attempted to conserve their finite resources by limiting family size through birth prevention or infanticide. In industrial
nations, too, a large number of children has often proved
burdensome. Today children usually survive to adulthood,
and only after prolonged and expensive dependency on the
family and society; this situation is in sharp contrast to the

productive participation of children in agricultural societies and in the early stages of industrial societies.

Unfortunately, life-extending medical achievements have not been paralleled by comparable achievements in the quality of life. The paradoxical discrepancies between lowered death rates and higher birth and survival rates, between greater knowledge of children's needs and deficient family and community resources for child health and development, between polluted and healthful environments, between medical knowledge and actual health care for all ages—all these discrepancies have encompassed the most crucial problems confronting postindustrial societies and societies wishing to industrialize. Curbing human reproduction quantitatively in favor of improving life qualitatively thus becomes an essential ingredient in any constructive narrowing of these discrepancies. This has been pointed out convincingly in the report of the National Commission on Population,[1] which documents carefully the many disadvantages of further population increases in the United States for the nation's families, its communities, and the national welfare. In its report the commission considered these broad issues at greater length than it considered the impact of contraception on the emotional aspects of sexual behavior and reproduction.

Essentially this book addresses itself to the need for humane reproduction in adjusting a nation to fulfillment of the capacities of its citizens and their communities. Specifically, it will address itself to the mental health aspects of controlled fertility. To be considered are the family's psychosocial and material resources; the impact of reproduction on the individual, on the family, and on communal functioning; and the implications for mental health of effective reproductive restraint, whether for the benefit of the family itself or for the purpose of population stabilization. The effects of reproductive behavior are circular: it is determined by, and in turn influences, sociocultural values as they relate to sex, to the care of the young, and to individual and communal mental health; reproductive restraint has an impact on all of these. This book endeavors to anchor these broad issues in clinical experience and research focusing on the individual, on the family, and on social systems. The problems involved in creating a numerically static society will be discussed and some of the predictable consequences of indefinite population growth described. Humane reproduction requires reproductive behavior and policies based on compassionate consideration of these issues, as well as action responsive to the needs of the individual, the family, and society beyond mere survival.

One purpose of this book is to show that the prevention of unwanted children is a significant factor in the promotion of mental health and the prevention of mental disorders— that there is hardly a single more effective tool for the prevention of emotional disorders than the prevention of unwanted pregnancies and unwanted parenthood.

At the outset a distinction must be made between family planning on the one hand and family limitation and population control on the other. The first involves planning by the partners of the size and composition of their particular family according to their own wishes, needs, and life goals. Such a plan may or may not dovetail with their own resources, their proficiency in sexual behavior, or the population policy of their society. Population control is an essentially political proposition which, as a policy, would impose the responsibility for reproductive restraint on everybody. In practice, family limitation has been effective in achieving population stability without any explicit policy: for example, in France for a century and a half following the Revolution of 1789, and in Ireland since the potato famine of the last century; in both nations, family limitation antedates modern contraceptives. In Japan population stability has been achieved in recent decades primarily through widespread abortion rather than by preventing conception.

Birth control methods, including abortion and sterilization, will be considered from the standpoint of mental health and optimal family health care. The starting point will be an examination of the essentials for healthful emotional growth in the context of family functioning because the family is the unit into which children are born. In almost all societies the family assumes or has been charged with the care of the young and their guidance into adulthood. The family must therefore be evaluated both as a concept and as an operational system in which family size is reconciled with effective family functioning and the requirements of society. This book will describe the basic functions of the family and the nature of the essential internal and external (communal) resources needed to assure its viability.

It will then consider the indications for limiting reproduction and its implications for the individual; the social pressures for population growth or limitation; and the resistances to humane reproduction encountered in the individual, the family, and the community.

Finally, it will outline educational principles for rational sexual behavior and family formation as essential elements in the achievement of humane reproduction and of parenthood based on choice and informed consent.

two

THE FAMILY AS A FUNCTIONING SYSTEM

Although the form and composition of the family may change over time and vary among different cultures, the family as an institution is characteristic of all human societies and of some animals. It seems to be determined by the biological given of two genders, only one of which can insure the survival of the newborn. The family serves to socialize children so that they become adults who fit into their society, a process called *enculturation*. Societies and their cultural continuity depend on the survival and enculturation of the young. The family as an institution seems to have evolved primarily for the rearing of the young; its function as a regulator of sexual activity seems by comparison quite secondary. Although sexual mores may vary greatly, ranging from monogamy to quite varied sexual interactions, strict parental role assignments are to be found in all societies. It is usually the biological parents who are charged with primary parental responsibility, although in some few societies collateral relatives or others may be assigned this role.

In Plato's day, in Seneca's, in the early Christian era, and in almost every century since, the decline and demise of the family as a viable institution has been an ever-recurring theme of historians, philosophers and other writers. Whether human history is viewed as a series of disasters or as a series of achievements in human collaboration, creativeness, and mastery over nature, family structure must be recognized as basic; the family has existed universally for as long as human history, and has been pointed to as the source of both good and evil.

Current divorce rates are sometimes cited as an indicator of the obsolescence of the family, but such figures are often misleading. Marriages are dissolved but families persist. At least three-fourths of all marriages in the United States remain intact, and almost half of single-parent families have resulted from the death of one parent. Moreover, as mental health professionals know only too well, the fact of no divorce does not vouch that all is healthy in a particular marriage or family, nor is divorce always undesirable for family health and welfare. When it is considered that the "average marriage life span" has doubled in this century, and that many of the legal, economic, social, and cultural barriers to divorce have been breached if not removed, the rise in the nation's divorce rate by one-third during the past half century is not very remarkable, related as it is to many determinants outside the family system. Although 83 percent of all children lived in two-parent homes in 1970, some 400,000 children in the

United States were affected by their parents' divorce in 1970, or 12 percent more than the national total for the year before.[1]

The survival of the family is quite remarkable when seen in the face of many social changes, the stresses of family nuclearity and isolation, and the economic liabilities currently facing parents, at least in Western and industrialized societies.

The perpetuation of the family as a social system is an indication of how essential the family is in humanizing the young, a function usually assigned to the biological parents. Single parents, adoptive parents, collateral relatives, or substitute parents (other adults) can fulfill the rearing tasks that guide a child into adulthood as defined by his society, but the family pattern has the advantage of providing two adults, as partners and as parents, to accomplish these tasks and is thus the mode that has been found most satisfactory in most cultures. The roles of partner and parent can be separated—not all societies cherish a monogamous family arrangement—but even in societies which sanction polygamy or extramarital sexual activity, the care of offspring is strictly regulated, and progeny are usually not sanctioned in extramarital alliances.

In monogamous families the marital relationship is central to the family dynamics and is just as important for the mutual satisfaction and support of the partners as it is for the tasks required in behalf of their children. This relationship, the *marital coalition*, must be effected by the couple as the first important family function, ideally before reproduction takes place.

The essential family functions performed by the marital coalition are nurturing tasks, enculturation of the young, emancipation of offspring from the family, and the creation of an environment in which leisure activities and crisis mastery can be developed. In many respects these tasks parallel the personality development of the child. These concepts of family functioning and task performance are based to some extent on the eight stages of development as defined by the well-known psychoanalyst and writer Erik H. Erikson and on the formulations of the sociologist Talcott Parsons concerning family structure and role divisions as models of social interaction.[2]

In the marital coalition the partners' interactions with each other form a structure which is developed at first to meet their mutual needs and satisfactions, and later to accommodate the dynamics of the family. The coalition must serve the developing needs of the children while protecting the exclusive mutual relationship of the parents. A central function of the coalition is sexual activity, forbidden to children within the family in almost all societies. Sexual activity is tied to reproduction in various ways; in one society it may be considered proper only for reproductive purposes, and in another it may be completely divorced from parental obligations. With the recent increase in life expectancy and decrease in infant mortality there is less tendency to regard the purpose of sexual activity as primarily reproductive. When childbearing is not desired or possible, the issues of sexual gratification and nongenerative sexual activity for mutual pleasure assume greater importance.

The achievement of mutual sexual gratification presupposes the partners' ability to communicate with each other about their desires and needs, including any desire or need for contraception.

Nonreproductive sex is in conflict with some traditions and religious teachings and with the needs and fantasies of many individuals. Marital discord can be precipitated when efforts are made to limit family size in the face of such beliefs. Likewise, when sexual intercourse is considered a marital duty, there are increased opportunities for marital dissension on both conscious and unconscious levels. The potential for inner and interpersonal conflict is an important variable in reproductive restraint and a common source of contraceptive failure even when there is a conscious wish not to have more children. Couples who have failed to achieve satisfying patterns of sexual intimacy apart from reproduction often experience contraceptive failure.

The spouses' intimacy is expressed both implicitly and explicitly in the sharing of feelings and in the conveying of respect and appreciation to each other, and of each other to the children and to outsiders. The representation of one partner by the other to the children is particularly important when one parent has to be absent periodically or permanently from the family. An important function of the marital coalition is the mutual reinforcement of the spouses' complementary sex-linked roles, so that each partner not only represents an appropriate identification model for the children, but each is reinforced in his marital and parental roles by the support and approval of the other.

Another function of the marital coalition is to define and establish the conjugal roles of the partners. In most cultures it is the activities of the male partner that determine the family's social position, with women being responsible for the affective and emotional climate in the family. These role divisions are not absolute, especially in modern American society, and parents may find task sharing more satisfactory than rigid division of roles on the basis of sex; young people in particular and women of all ages are challenging traditional stereotypes. Role allocations and decision-making methods in a marriage vary among different socioeconomic classes in the same society. In regard to both psychological and social development, the division of family tasks the parents develop usually determines what kind of group the family will become. In any case, as the ages of family members change, so must their roles in the family. In terms of power and decision making, it has been shown that health care is more satisfactory and health standards are higher when decision making is joint and not the province of one parent.[3]

The marital coalition must serve the establishment of triangular relationships after children are born. These "triangles" must be flexible, as each newborn must be very close to the mother, absorbing a great deal of her attention and energy. The older family members must adapt to this new requirement. The older child must give up his primary closeness with his mother in favor of the newcomer and must learn to tolerate his replacement by a younger sibling. A successful marital coalition is essential to successful adjustment of the children within the growing family.

In contrast to work groups or therapy groups, the family group operates on the basis of a predetermined evolutionary history with rather distinct age-related tasks in accordance with certain biological, psychological, and social functions. Role modification within the family over time is therefore a necessity; it also demonstrates to children that there are times when the welfare of the group overrides individual needs and times when the individual's needs take precedence over the welfare of the group. Parental role allocations are important models to the child of how the two sexes divide family tasks and how they differ in their attitudes. They also prepare the child for peer group relationships.

Ideally, in modern American society, an understanding of these phenomena would be reflected in the behavior of all parents-to-be. Reproduction would be consciously and jointly planned, undertaken only after consideration of the responsibilities involved and regardless of the ultimate number of children desired. A distinction must be made between wanted children and planned children; surveys show that the majority of firstborns are unplanned but usually "wanted" once the baby is born, even when the pregnancy occurred premaritally (as it does in at least 40 percent of teenage marriages).[4] The fact of having a child at a certain time is no indication of proper understanding or readiness for parenthood. Some young people can adapt to the responsibilities of parenthood if the nine months of gestation can be utilized as a period of emotional growth and maturation, as in the case of those aided by special prenatal care programs for teenage mothers-to-be.[5] The disadvantages of premature parenthood will be considered later in this book.

Nurturing the Young

Nurturing tasks are traditionally assigned to the mother, although she can perform them best when supported tangibly and emotionally by her partner. These tasks include not only the providing of food but the psychological aspects of feeding. Primary among them is the establishment of basic trust. Early nurturing of the child involves helping him learn how to manage and control his body and how to observe, distinguish between, and communicate about his inner and external experiences, even before he speaks. It entails furnishing him appropriate stimulus experiences and learning opportunities. Parents must understand that play is the young child's work. The importance of these nurturing functions in the child's early life has been recognized clearly only in recent times. The potential damage to personality development, social adjustment, and educational capabilities when these nurturing tasks beyond feeding are not adequately fulfilled is currently a source of concern and an object of investigation.

Weaning is also a nurturing task, and involves more than merely withdrawing the bottle or breast. The intense physical closeness with the mother must be loosened and in its stead an essentially nonphysical intimacy established with all family members. The process of weaning, which is usually the first separation experience of the child, determines his sense of separateness and his acquisition of ego boundaries.

Mastery of separation can be defined as follows: The child

experiences the pain of losing the supportive closeness to a significant person (the parent) without losing faith and trust in the continuity of the relationship or in the ultimate restoration of good feeling and a sense of security. Through separation experiences the child learns and grows—he becomes better able to avoid the same impasse that confronted him the first time and less vulnerable to or threatened by subsequent separations from others. This mastery must be facilitated by the opportunity to observe, imitate, and eventually internalize the modes of other family members in coping with frustration and separation anxiety, and also in mourning the permanent loss of a relative or friend.

Enculturation

Any clear line between nurturing and enculturating tasks is arbitrary, as family functions are continuous and overlap. Nevertheless, passage of the oedipal phase (usually by about the age of five) may be considered a turning away from the earlier nurturing experiences toward those of enculturation. At this point, the child will usually have achieved body control and gender awareness, will have acquired verbal competence, and will have accepted the incest taboo in the sense of feeling comfortable in his relationship to each parent. The period of latency then begins about age five or six and extends to puberty. During this period, sexual and erotic strivings and problems are at a minimum. The child is freed for instrumental learning and for increasing his capacity to invest in peer relationships. He is allowed greater distance from the family circle at the same time that he is taught within the family many of the instrumental modes of his culture in shared work and games.

Together with the child's formal instruction, the family continues to inculcate the communicative and social skills and interactional modes of its culture, defining the norms of relationships both explicitly and by example. The style of communication and the competence of the family in communicating are crucial. Significant deviation from culturally valid patterns of interaction, symbolization, and reality concepts can create disturbances within the family and handicap its members, especially the young members, in relating to the surrounding community.

Emancipation from the Family

In industrial societies, stepping into adulthood usually means physical and geographical separation as well as psychological and social emancipation from one's family of origin. To be accomplished successfully, this final separation cannot be abrupt—it must be the culmination of many psychosocial differentiations between parents and child. The first steps toward independence which the family must encourage as the child moves through his developmental stages are school attendance, identification with a peer group outside the family, and living-away-from-home experiences (summer camps, for example); later steps include social activities with the opposite sex (such as dating) and jobs (or college). Finally, his achievement of a social identity and self-direction culminates in readiness for marriage and parenthood. Successful completion of these steps calls for developmental resources and opportunities outside the family.

Emancipation from the family demands mutual tolerance and resilience between the generations. Adolescents need to experiment with independent behavior and often teeter between their still intense needs for dependency and guidance and their equally intense strivings for independence, at times annoyingly proclaimed. Currently, youth's experimental independence often involves early sexual activity leading to family conflict rather than considered family discussions of responsible sexual activity and reproduction. Unfortunately, Western families have remained handicapped in communicating and guiding effectively in this area.

Emancipation may be precipitated by marriage or pregnancy. Today this is probably always unhealthful for the young parents, as it usually foreshortens further education and preparation for a career. It often means flight from the family of origin and failure to master psychosocial independence. Certainly it is not an auspicious beginning for a new generation.

The child's experimentation with independence often expresses much hostility against the older generation. Parents must meet this hostility together, and they also must prepare at this time to live again as a dyad. Emancipation thus entails the evolutionary dissolution of the family as a unit because grandparental functions are limited and are not continuous in the nuclear family of industrial societies.

Family Environment

Family sharing of leisure and recreation is essential in all societies. Television, communal playgrounds, and the mobility often afforded youth today have rendered family group play and joint recreational activity with other families seemingly superfluous. Yet there is a deficiency in family functioning when family games and work projects are replaced entirely by solitary pursuit of separate concerns on the part of each family member. Joint meals become a rarity in such households. Because work, including formal schooling, has to be different for each family member, such family projects as games, outings, and the like are all the more crucial for family interaction and as learning models for intimate non-and-take. The creation of an environment in which individuals can function with less psychological defensiveness than in the larger society is an important family function. All adults can be masters in their own home, but only a few can be masters in their work. At home, children can be accorded greater tolerance for their foibles and more guidance in overcoming them than they can be afforded at school or elsewhere. The family, no matter how constituted, must provide for emotional and psychological recuperation, the way station for recharging the batteries that power the children's and the parents' participation in community life.

The four major parental task capabilities—nurturing, enculturation, emancipation, and the creation of an environment conducive to growth—should be evaluated when procreation and the number of offspring are being decided. Without an understanding of these tasks, family planning is meaningless and informed consent for truly humane parenthood is beyond the capabilities of the young parents-to-be.

three | # FAMILY STRESSES IN MODERN INDUSTRIAL SOCIETY

The burdens on the isolated nuclear family in industrial and postindustrial societies are psychosocial, economic, and ecological. In an industrial society, families are usually of two generations. The father is absent during most of the young child's waking hours, and household help for the mother is uneconomical in most families. This leaves many mothers during the day with the complete responsibility for child rearing, especially in the case of the preschool child. The full-time housewife-mother role is a recent phenomenon. But once a mother, a woman may have more and more children as a substitute for the career she was denied by her first child. In the past, women on the farm and in the city did their work while caring for their children; it was both together, not a division between "productive" work and housekeeping. Today, although men can share household burdens and many do, such sharing is limited in a basically competitive society where fulfilling one's potential often requires of the father long hours of work and application on the job, usually out-side the home. A career in itself can prevent his participation, not to mention moonlighting for economic reasons. From the standpoint of mental health, consistent yet flexible division of tasks and the assumption of complementary roles are more important than any fixed assignment of chores on a quantitative basis. Task sharing is also pleasurable. Yet the urban and suburban family group is held together more by affectional bonds and intangible sharing than by the actual need to share work and leisure that characterized rural families of the past.

Social models to relieve stress. Although special arrangements to relieve full-time mothering are relatively new in the United States, they are well established in Israel and Russia, among other countries, in the form of day care centers. Such centers are not only important for mothers who work, but they enrich the lives of the children who attend them, as do playground programs and camping opportunities. Regular exposure to adults other than one's parents is important in providing alternate identification models; day care centers can be viewed as a modern part-replacement of the earlier ex-tended family system from among whose members support figures and substitute parents were easily procured.

Experimentation with communal living may add to the limited resources currently available for effective child care services that benefit the child while reducing parental burdens for some families. Parents in communes generally can spell each other in parental work assignments. Whereas communal living has some of the advantages of an extended family system, and also provides alternate adult models for children in a two-generation system, it probably has the disadvantages of an extended family in that conflicts of sibling rivalry attend the sharing of resources.

Since 1920 the United States has changed from a half rural nation to one that is 80 percent urban. This change has caused complex tasks and special stresses peculiar to the isolated nuclear family. In the light of these developments the family has proved remarkably adaptive as the primary institution of socialization and as the resilient buffer system between the developing child and a complex postindustrial society. Although clinicians in particular are aware of the existence of many unsatisfactory families, the inadequacy of education and support for family life, combined with the high cost of untimely fertility and the frequency of ill-advised family formation, makes the success and endurance of the family as an institution all the more notable.

To Be or Not to Be a Parent

Little is known about how people, married or unmarried, make decisions for family formation—whether to have a family, how many children to have, and when to have them.[1] However, a good deal is known, at least statistically, about the proportion of unplanned pregnancies, if not of unwanted children.[2] As Thackeray once reflected, "If people only made prudent marriages, what a stop to population there would be." Were the advice implicit in his comment seriously considered, especially by young people, unwanted reproduction and overpopulation might be reduced. Only severe economic pressures have forced people in the United States and other nations to limit procreation to a replacement figure of 2.1 children per couple. In the 1930s, under the impact of financial depression, the two-child family was preferred by a majority and had become typical in the United States. During the 25 years following World War II, however, the three- to four-child family was preferred. These levels have been dropping again and only recently were reported to be at 2.5 children per family,[3] with only 20 percent of adults wanting families with four or more children.[4]

Aside from the psychosocial considerations, family formation is affected by such tangible factors as economics, housing, and career opportunities for both spouses, as well as by the resources and limitations of the larger community. On the whole these are likely to be taken into account only by young couples from the middle and upper classes. Yet there is a clear need to extend career opportunities to wives from all classes lest they embark on the career of housewife and mother by default, rather than by conscious and deliberate choice. This is important not only for a sound ecology but for the mental health of women. It is not necessary that menopausal women be left without a meaningful, satisfying life composed of more than shopping and housekeeping for two. The shift in values which has rejected the career of housewife as inadequate for a lifetime is prerequisite to achievement of family size limitation on a national scale.

Unprepared parenthood. Although Americans have practiced reproductive restraint, as in the depression of the thirties, they have a poor record of personal decision-making for parenthood. In 1960, two-thirds of couples with children reported using no method of birth control before arrival of the first child. From 1961 to 1965 the average interval between marriage and first birth was 18 months excluding fetal deaths, but one-third of all first births were premarital conceptions and 42 percent of teenage mothers were delivered within eight months of marriage.[5]

Unplanned first pregnancies in particular usually indicate parenthood without informed decision to become a parent. Postponing the first pregnancy and entering parenthood with forethought and consent would serve the goals of physical and mental health and a sound ecology. Postponement of accidental first pregnancies alone would increase significantly the average parental age at first birth, and increase the number of nonparents at all ages, while resulting in better child spacing for the nation's families.

In 1968, the latest year for which full statistics are available, 900,000, or almost 25 percent, of the 3.5 million births in the United States occurred to mothers under 22. A large percentage of these births were unplanned. In view of the demands upon parents today, postponement of motherhood to age 22 is recommended. In 1968, one out of four births would have been postponed had this recommendation been observed. Unmarried motherhood had increased between 1940 and 1967 as follows: a two-and-one-half-fold increase among those aged 20 to 24 and more than fivefold among those aged

25 or older. This represents a rise from 3.7 to 8.4 percent of all births. It is noteworthy that the illegitimacy rate in the white population has risen 30 percent since 1960, whereas the rate for nonwhites declined 7 percent in the same period.[6] Added to these figures should be the number of "legal" but probably unplanned births resulting from premarital conceptions. In the late sixties an opposite trend became noticeable— a reduction in the percentage of illegitimate births (but not necessarily of out-of-wedlock pregnancies), probably due to the greater availability of abortion.[7]

The number of lifelong nonparents in the nation, currently about 7 percent, is small compared with the highest rate, 18 percent of married women born from 1900 to 1910, whose most fertile years coincided with the depression. Currently 96 percent of people marry, half the women before age 21. Of these couples, 92 percent have children, and a high rate of marital vicissitude and family breakup may be inevitable. Lifelong marriage, with or without children, can be a joyous experience without parallel, or it can be miserable. The same is true of parenthood. In order to reduce the personal and social tragedies of disturbed family life and the misery of unwanted children born to unprepared, unwilling parents, it is necessary to prevent marriage and parenthood that result from accident or the mere desire to conform. The presence of 500,000 children in foster homes or institutions suggests that, in addition to the 6 percent of nonparents in the United States, a large number of biological parents do not welcome or cannot cope with parenthood. Many biological mothers have not had the privilege or opportunity for informed consent to parenthood. The recent experience following legalization of abortion and the rise in age at first marriage hold promise that people are becoming more aware of the personal and social responsibilities of marriage and parenthood and are making more deliberate choices. However, the option for nonparenthood is still too often foreclosed by a combination of uterine and ideological misconceptions, with childless couples openly pitied or made to feel guilty for their failure to reproduce.

Adoptive parenthood. The decision for parenthood is most clear-cut in the case of adoption. But adopted children are handicapped by a number of factors. First of all, their biological mothers usually did not want them. Probably even more important are the socially induced difficulties of adoptive parenthood. For decades adoptive parents have been taught and have taught their children that there are two kinds of parents, *real* and *adoptive*. Then came the concept of *birth* and *real* parents. Giving birth may be beautiful, but it is secondary as far as the child is concerned—it is the animal part of parenthood; the human part is rearing the child. For the child, the parents who raise him are his real parents. Indeed, the chief reason a child need know he was adopted is to give him a medical history containing needed genetic information; a secondary reason is that he may find out from others what he is not told by his adoptive parents. Society's exaggerated concern with biological parenthood is reflected in the one-time recommendation by some adoption agencies that the children they placed be brought to the agency on their birthday so that they would be perfectly clear about their origin.

The adoption issue is important in another context: In a psychological utopia, one could argue that anyone who is not ready to adopt a child is not ready for parenthood at all. To this day, however, adoption is treated as second-class parenthood. Society demands the right to screen infertile couples for their qualifications to rear children, whereas fertile couples are presumed to be capable of competent parenthood.

Another socially engendered disadvantage for infertile adoptive parents derives from the general attitude of pity toward childless couples. This attitude puts infertile couples under pressure to adopt, when in the absence of such pressure they might have opted for a childless marriage.

With increased family planning and recourse to abortion the number of unwanted children to be placed for adoption should be reduced to the minimum. Already there is a shortage of white children in this group, so that white childless couples are faced with a choice of doing without children or adopting nonwhite children. That a growing number of couples are making such adoptions with courage, competence, and love may profoundly affect society's attitudes toward race as well as toward parenthood.

Until recently adoption as an alternative way to form a family was an unusual step, seldom taken except in cases of biological incapacity. Today more and more people are adopting children by prior initiative or just plain love for children. In some states unmarried persons may adopt. Homosexual couples may want to be parents, and this would necessitate a change in values on the part of society at large. If the state allows anybody who can get pregnant to become a

parent and takes no child away from a parent except for con-
spicuous neglect or severe abuse, is there justification for
denying adoption to any adult who wants to be a parent?

Stresses on Women

The issue of women's roles in modern society is a complex
and controversial one. The demand for equality of the sexes
in every walk of life is not about to affect the unique capacity
of women to bear children. Although femininity is largely a
culturally defined characteristic, it is also embedded in biological forces. Pregnancy and suckling of the young still call
for role divisions between the parents, whether or not protection from predators during these phases is a real necessity. In
terms of mental and bodily needs, breast-feeding may be more
important for mothers than it is for babies.

While regenerative cloning (asexual reproduction) and
extrauterine fetal development can be envisioned in principle,
neither is likely to become the preferred form of reproduction in the foreseeable future. Furthermore, parenthood is not
just a set of tasks, but an essential ingredient in a meaningful
life providing creative opportunity to many if not most adults.
While an equal division of parental functions is theoretically
possible, it is unfeasible in a culture that offers career advancement primarily to those who work full time.

The housewife-mother career. Housekeeping and child
care as life goals are realistic now only for those women past

40 or 50 who are prepared and willing to continue this calling in behalf of other people's children and families. Reciprocal family functioning must give opportunities for the personal growth and emotional health of all its members, parents as well as children. One of the sacrifices of an overburdened family scene is a growing relationship between the spouses that permits intimacy and sexual expression. A common complaint of married women with children is that sexual intercourse is perfunctory and boring, however frequent. Such fatigue or ennui may also play a role in contraceptive failure (taking a a chance might relieve boredom).

One of the choices confronting women is whether to seek motherhood at all. Society does not deal kindly with spinsters and infertile couples, yet nonparenthood is compatible with mental health and a productive, satisfying life.

Another choice concerns the reconciliation of motherhood with work or career. Some compromises have to be made unless the mother is prepared to leave the care of even the very young to a substitute mother. Yet democratic industrial societies have denigrated substitute mothering and the housekeeper role to such a degree that it is rarely practical economically or possible operationally for a mother to work full time and be satisfied that her family does not suffer by her absence from the home. A tandem solution is sometimes possible. Women can finish their education or achieve certain career goals before undertaking motherhood and then return to work or profession after the youngest child is ready for a day care center or kindergarten. Obviously this solution implies that the community will provide the necessary facilities for young children, and appropriate work conditions for mothers. Without them a woman may see little choice but to become a full-time parent, continuing on and on with pregnancy and motherhood, since there is no hope of escape from parental and home chores in any case. However, it must be recognized that motivations for pregnancy and for motherhood are no more identical for all women than are their capacities for either.

The issue of women's role in contemporary society is crucial to the formation of small families. The confinement of women to the home and discrimination against women in employment have been rationalized up to the present time by ancient myth and prejudicial habit. The Nineteenth Amendment granted women political equality; with the abolition of restrictive abortion laws, women are being extended the right to decide for themselves whether or not and when to become mothers. Without the opportunity to obtain an abortion when she does not want motherhood, a woman's freedom to guide her own fate does not exist. In this respect, many nations that are otherwise considered authoritarian and oppressive are more libertarian than the United States.[8]

The abortion controversy reveals many outmoded beliefs and attitudes about women and femininity. As in other areas of discrimination, ingrained attitudes and prejudices do not yield readily to reason and rational education, and in consequence often bring forth aggressive and overstated demands from the oppressed. From the mental health standpoint, as well as in the cause of justice, the nation can ill afford to continue abridging the rights of whole groups, whose members thus become surly and coerced participants in the society. An unwilling mother who was refused an abortion is a victim of oppressive prejudice and discrimination.

Stresses from and on Unwanted Children

There are few psychiatric case histories that do not reveal in some way the patient's sense of not having been wanted, regardless of his parents' opinion in the matter. There are also a good many patients whose family, when observed and studied carefully, shows evidence of not having wanted in some significant way the particular child who became the patient. Moreover, it is clear that the tens of thousands of children who are known to suffer physical abuse at the hands of at least one parent are only the visible top of an iceberg of "unwantedness." There are many intangible forms of making children feel unwanted in the emotional and psychosocial areas of life; in these cases, as well as in cases of gross mistreatment, the children may have been wanted at birth or before.

It is important to distinguish between two types of unwanted children. One is the child who to begin with was not wanted by one parent or the other, or was found unsatisfactory later on for whatever reason. The other type is the child who may have been wanted by his parents and his family but is not wanted by society because the family is overburdened and cannot give him the care and training all children need. Society at large is not prepared to provide substitute parenting, except for that minority of unwanted babies who are offered for, and are desirable for, adoption. The child who is not wanted in the family into which he was born is the concern of this section; the child unwanted by society will be discussed in the following section.

It takes an unwanting parent to produce an unwanted child. The fact of being consciously unwilling to be a mother is signal and stark, though the reasons for this hard fact are legion. Ambivalence is no stranger to the woman who wants her baby, but this distinct, other feeling of not wanting a pregnancy is too certain to be ambivalent. It is an attitude compounded of dismay, frustration, and anger; it is the attitude of the woman whose baby represents blasted hopes and ruined plans, lost chances and missed opportunities, dropping out of school and rushing into a precipitous, ill-considered marriage. It afflicts unwed teenage mothers and middle-aged mothers ready to turn to other things; it permeates whole families under stress of increased family size, decreased family resources, and the endless unhappy consequences of one life too many. This "unwanting" is too well grounded to be dissolved by the charm of a new baby.

An unwanted pregnancy—unplanned, untimely, accidental, unwelcome—makes a pregnant woman unfriendly and implacable toward her baby; and however much guilt and conflict these feelings may cause her, they do not compare to the hostile, resentful, condemning attitudes that are in store for the child. No family can contain such a malignant relationship without every member's suffering.

Baby care takes a willing heart. To the simple transaction of nursing, an infant brings utter dependency and vulnerability. Everything has to be done for him. His mother's feelings introduce him to his beginning life. The quality of his mother's care becomes a part of his dawning consciousness and brings a response in kind. Gentleness breeds ease and trust; impatience breeds discomfort and distrust.

The unwanted child senses his mother's anger, hostility, and resentment toward him. He does not know why she feels as she does and cannot avoid his own responding feelings of anxiety and tension. He lives at the center of conflict, the breeding place of emotional disturbance.

The fate of an unwanted child whose mother has repressed her feelings of rejection, or whose father disapproves of the mother as a mother, is equally thorny. For such a child the prize of approval seems a possibility but he feels his efforts to attain it are unsuccessful. He will blame himself for his failures long before he finally understands the true source of his inevitable lack of success, why he can never win.

To be wanted, to be welcome, is basic to the beginnings of all successful human relationships. A sympathetic understanding between two people helps to minimize the hazards of tension and conflict. The life history of an unwanted child demonstrates the truth that no good can come from dislike and rejection.

Although the exact differences between wanted and unwanted children cannot be scientifically established, it is safe to say that wanted children are rarely found in welfare shelters or foster homes. Wanted children are less likely to be found on pediatric wards suffering from neglect, broken bones, or physical abuse. Wanted children rarely become wards of society, dependent upon the advocacy of society's overburdened agencies to keep them from becoming street children. Wanted children do not become well known to all the categories of professionals who specialize in helping children emotionally and socially.

If an unwanted baby, having survived the period of pregnancy, does not die at birth or suffer additional physical or mental handicap, he may collapse early in life into a mental illness which removes him from the arena of daily life and relieves him of having to cope with it. His illness slams the door on communication not only with his parents but with all people. This unwanted child retires from life.

The less sick fight back. Feeling hated, they hate—taught by hate to hate. Unable to please, ignored, despised, the unwanted child will fight for attention even though provocative, offensive behavior brings on further disapproval and punishment. At least it brings attention. In this way unwanted children who stay in the arena of daily affairs will range themselves gradually along a well-documented scale of unproductive, unrewarding behavior patterns that lead only to lifetime trouble.

With no hope of winning approval at home, the unwanted child becomes accustomed to receiving disapproval. He then behaves in a self-fulfilling predictive manner—first at home, then in school, and finally in society. Followed far enough, this road leads to ingrained antisocial behavior. A lifelong distrust of society's ability to be fair places a person outside the laws of that society. The outlaw makes his own unrealistic, self-serving rules of conduct, which inevitably outrage and alienate society. This is his revenge. He is ignored, poorly nurtured, neglected, exploited, and abused. These are the overt signs of unwantedness, visible to anyone. Worst of all, the hurts of feeling insignificant, unloved, and unlovable are survived only at the cost of scarring his personality.

All mental disorders or brain damage are not rooted in unwantedness, but the contribution unwantedness makes to these complex conditions is preventable. Mental health specialists from every discipline know how the lives of unwanted children are blighted and realize that these children do not have a fair and equal opportunity to grow and prosper. This knowledge can be translated into responsible action; it is humane and possible for all human beings to choose to have only wanted children.

When a couple prevents a conception they are not able or willing to foster, they are acting humanely, rationally, and maturely. They are preventing an unwanted child. If conception occurs and they still feel unable or unwilling to raise a child, their responsibility is to have an abortion or arrange for an adoption. In either case they are preventing an unwanted child. Outraged sensibilities of others have to be put in balance with the fate of unwanted children. Everyone should know that the life of an unwanted child is unenviable. The responsibility of society for a child does not begin or end with birth. A child needs parents who are responsible enough to plan to have him when they are able to give him a fair chance to grow and prosper. In addition, he needs a community that supports his family.

Stresses from and on Society

Although society proclaims that all children should have equal care and opportunity, the phenomenon of socially unwanted children remains ominous and documentable. The evidence points to a society unconcerned with its children, which cares little about and neglects specifically those children who become its responsibilities. At least 300,000 unwanted children are known to reside in usually unsatisfactory foster homes or institutions, awaiting disposition by adoption which is not likely to eventuate.[9] Community services for all children—education, and health and welfare services—are also inadequate and are the first to be curtailed still further when governmental economies are instituted. It is difficult to maintain the illusion of a society concerned with its children in which upwards of half a million children are underattended and sometimes mistreated in institutions or foster homes.

Justine Wise-Polier, former justice of the New York City Family Court, has pointed out the disparity between the myth of a child-centered society and the reality of indiscriminate budget cuts affecting services for children in courts, institutions, and schools.[10] Services for delinquent youth have been equally hampered despite the intense nationwide concern with crime in the streets and the violence engendered by drug addiction. Children requiring psychiatric hospital care often have suffered from faulty or misguided rearing; in the hospital setting they also suffer from therapeutic neglect and the squalid living conditions frequently found in public institutions. It is easy to blame the institutions—medical care systems, school systems, the police, and so on—but everyone in the society is to blame.

A family usually assumes that when it balances its budget it is "taking care of itself" and would do better if only taxes were not so exorbitant. Yet it is taxes which pay for public institutions, and few if any families with children pay fully for what they receive. It is estimated that it costs a family $25,000 to rear a child to legal maturity with a good education.[11] For example, in a typical town the annual public school tuitions are calculated at $500 per child, or $6,500 over the period of a child's primary and secondary education. However, the average annual tax contribution per household to the school operation in the same town is barely half this amount, so that a family with three children would only be paying between 15 and 20 percent of its own schooling costs during that period, exclusive of other services. Even in a purely economic sense families are often uninformed about what their children actually cost and to what extent they depend on the community—that is, on all taxpayers. When a child has to be reared outside of the home by institutional arrangements, the cost is over $100,000 by the time he is 18—usually for inadequate and inferior care. Indirectly and intangibly, society contributes a good portion of the differential between what the family of a child pays and the actual expenditures for his care.

Next to the family, schools provide for a child's development and mental health. Currently there is considerable resistance among taxpayers to meeting school expenses; from the mental health standpoint this resistance intensifies the effects of inadequate and discriminatory school arrangements. Although an ever-increasing demand is put on the schools, in terms of both education and special services, many of them related to mental health, such as guidance, remedial reading and the like, many school systems are forced to curtail existing operations, and these special services ("the frills") are usually the first to go. In 1971 over half the school bond referendums in the United States met majority voter disapproval. One of the likely victims of "economy" campaigns is adequate family life and sex education in the schools, often a source of controversy. While recent surveys show that only a minority of young people at first intercourse expect a continuing relationship, at least a third of them use no contraception.[12]

There is a connection between the dissatisfaction of many young people with school programs and the fact that the peak year in which single mothers produce their firstborn is 18, thereby cutting short for many of them any further education and the pursuit of desirable life goals. This is true whether their babies are wanted or not. (In fact, some youngsters use pregnancy for relationship coinage.) But pregnancy wishes must not be equated with readiness for parenthood or motivation for it.[13]

It also holds true for married young parents that a birth within two years of marriage is associated with poorer marital adjustment[14] and with more problems for the child than is the case when children are born after the first two years of marriage.[15] Premature parenthood is bad for parents, for marriages, and for children—therefore it cannot be good for society.

Family Size as a Source of Stress

It is hard to imagine a more important variable in preventive psychiatry than family planning. No close rival or substitute has been found for good parenting—an arduous and joyful task when undertaken willingly, an arduous and soul-destroying burden when not wanted. In general it appears that small families do better than large ones, and that babies reasonably spaced and born to mature women develop better than others not so favored. It also appears that, poverty aside, poor physical and mental health mark the large family regardless of social class.

For instance, 70 percent of military recruits rejected for mental health reasons come from families of four children or more although they represent only 33 percent of the nation's families. This is not a static correlation inasmuch as recruits who have five or more siblings represent only 11 percent of families nationwide, but almost half of them (47 percent) are rejected from service for the same reasons. In another instance 59 percent of inmates in one reformatory had four or more siblings. Unfortunately, the class distribution of these cohorts is not known, although poverty, with the attendant undernourishment and limited socialization, has doubtless contributed significantly to these figures.[16]

Other studies have demonstrated that intelligence and educational achievement correlate inversely with a pupil's family size regardless of social class.[17] Women with many pregnancies exhibit a clinical syndrome called "maternal fatigue" and demonstrate increments in complications of pregnancy and delivery together with a decrease in the health and developmental status of the younger children from birth onward.[18]

While small family size may not inevitably favor mental health and social adjustment, it is significant that 70 percent of children coming from large families desire small families for themselves, whereas the reverse is not true. A study of 400 psychiatric inpatients revealed some challenging correlations concerning child spacing and sibling relationships.[19] Patients born within two years of an older sibling had a disproportionate incidence of paranoid conditions; those with a younger sibling born within two years of their own birth had a disproportionate incidence of psychopathy.

Most studies in this area report nothing specific about wantedness as a variable. Yet it has been observed that not only the unwanted child but the entire family suffers from his presence. One study has compared an "unwanted" birth sample (whose mothers sought but were denied abortion) with a random sample of births; the abortion seekers' children did worse with respect to their health and social adjustment in the ensuing 21 years than did their controls.[20] If feeling wanted is a measurable factor in mental health, it will eventually be detected. As the population of newborns changes from mostly unplanned to mostly planned—in number and spacing—mental health will eventually improve. So far, this transition has not been socioeconomically uniform. The poor, the less educated, and the very young mothers have more unplanned children than their favored counterparts, so that great social and professional effort will be required to equalize the important advantages of planned family formation.

The best indicator of success in family planning over the short run will be found in statistics on maternal and infant mortality and on the incidence of disease among newly born babies. In these respects the United States has lagged behind a dozen other Western countries. If predictions based on recent studies prove valid, a decrease in birth defects, cerebral palsy, minimal brain dysfunction, and behavioral disorders will occur as a result of better family planning, nutrition, and prenatal care.[21] Women who eagerly wish to have children are more likely to take care of themselves during gestation than unhappily pregnant women, who have been known to abuse themselves in the hope of aborting the pregnancy. Unfortunately there can be little doubt that more children are abused to death than are removed by courts from abusive parents.[22] This situation is likely to improve as children become scarcer and accordingly become more valued by parents, the community, and the larger society.

Other considerations point to the desirability of small families, quite apart from population pressures. While many people want as many children "as they can afford," this affording usually has been perceived only in an economic sense. "Affording" must also mean what people can afford in terms of their own emotional and cultural resources and of the community support systems available for the care of their children. A couple solely occupied with child care finds little energy and time for marital intimacy and satisfaction, let alone personal growth and further adult education.

Adult education was of little moment when the average life expectancy was less than 50 years, the situation prevailing early in this century. Since then, however, life expectancy has increased by some 25 years. The health and quality of life of a couple during these last 25 years are as essential a personal and social concern as are the health and welfare of the family with dependent children. A couple whose entire attention and emotional resources for 20 to 30 years have been devoted to children are ill equipped to find equivalent satisfaction when returning to their own more restricted interactions. Nor is it likely that women who have been full-time housewives and mothers for that long can suddenly, upon finding themselves almost unemployed at home, undertake other meaningful and productive activities in a society that does not look kindly on middle-aged or elderly job seekers.

Admittedly, children in small families can be disadvantaged when poor transportation and neighborhood planning, combined with rigid age stratification in schools, tend to isolate them. The school systems could promote some type of age mixing, perhaps through the tutoring of younger children by older children; day care centers located in high schools could provide a needed service while teaching future parents about child development. An only child would benefit from such arrangements. The one-child family is least popular, even though indications are that "only" children perform better by all the usual measures of achievement than other children. The prejudice against the one-child family is unwarranted.[23] The prospect of preplanning the sex of a child could also contribute to the goal of small families.

The move to the commune is interesting, and doubtless valuable for some people, temporarily if not permanently. Some communes could be said to be better environments for children than some families—which is not to herald the commune as the successor to the nuclear family. It is a minority phenomenon, not so widespread as its notoriety suggests. However, it could have the effect of raising the average age of (conventional) marriage for young people, possibly a wholesome development in view of the fact that "young" marriages fail disproportionately often.[24] In one long-established commune pattern, the Israeli kibbutz, parents have a daily two-hour period with their children, more parental time than many children enjoy in nuclear families.

The late 1960s may have marked a turning point for the family in the United States, showing two reversals: a downward trend in birthrate and an upward trend in the age of marriage. These same years also witnessed an upsurge in concern about the environment and its pollution by people, with a focus on people as pollutants. Today there is, at least among educated youth, a marked concern about careless reproduction. A distinction is being made between living together and making a permanent marital or family commitment, which may bespeak an attitude that "the family is dead—long live the family." What may be dead or at least dying is family formation by accident, or family formation for the purpose of sanctioning sexual relationships or accidental pregnancy.

four | # POPULATION CONTROLS: TWO DISCIPLINES AGREE

As the National Commission on Population Growth and the American Future pointed out in 1972,[1] it can no longer be assumed that no matter how many children are produced they will somehow be taken care of and somehow flourish. Such assumptions slant history to suit human ideals, based as they are on pride in a society that has grown enormously in size, in utilization of resources, and in material production. Yet continued production of people at recent rates can lead to disaster. The increase in the number of human beings on earth has become one of the major crises facing man today.[2]

Enhanced death control effected by the medical profession and the health sciences has shifted the age structure of populations to the point where in many regions of both developed and developing countries the large numbers of dependent young and old hinder economic development and accommodation to social and technological change. Malnourishment and famine are very much in evidence and are likely to spread in the near future, even as societies strive for a higher standard of living. Meanwhile, the transformation of natural resources into material goods, with the attendant pollution of air, land, and water, menaces the balance of the biosphere. The crisis in ecology is threatening man and his cultures. Spreading urbanization, coupled with increasing mobility and the rapid pace of social change, further aggravates the difficulties facing a burgeoning population.

Ecology and psychiatry, perhaps the earliest and most recent of the life-oriented disciplines to become concerned with the population problem, share a crisis-oriented concern and focus. Both disciplines systematically study phenomena of change—the growth and decline of certain systems—in attempting to discover the determinants and the governing forces of change and their interconnections. The crisis in the psychosocial field requires an emotional readjustment and rebalancing of relationships.[3] Similarly ecologists appreciate how once-stable communities and populations can adaptively rearrange their functions and relationships toward a new stability characterized by new organizational patterns.

Rarely do animal populations maintain numerical stability over many generations. Low numbers of predators and an absence of disease, combined with an abundance of food and favorable weather, conspire to permit rapid increase in numbers until stress from territorial constraints and too-frequent social interaction, as well as unusual weather or overuse of food resources, all contribute to a rapid decline in numbers. Thus, natural populations customarily fluctuate about some intermediate density which ecologists designate as *the carry-*

ing capacity of the environment. In considering this broad picture, the search is for general principles explaining the dynamics of the relationships among large numbers of individuals.

By contrast, psychiatrists as crisis managers have only recently looked beyond the individual toward those more complex processes of community ecology and evolution that contribute meaning and at times stress to the individual's life. Though overpopulation by man is patently a crisis in the making, and both ecology and psychiatry are crisis disciplines, each discipline suffers from its own historical myopia in evaluating the problem perceived by both. Without mutual correction of vision, these disciplines will contribute little to alleviate it.

Erik Erikson and the English biologist Julian Huxley made significant contributions toward fusing the philosophies of evolution and ecology on the one hand, and those of psychology and psychoanalysis on the other, as they bear upon the population crisis.[4] Their essays and formulations suggest that the search for identity and the fulfillment of one's potential stand at the core of the human state. Such fulfillment requires satisfaction of generativity, an extension of sexuality. Duplication of the biological self through the production and rearing of children satisfies the generative drive at its primary and basic level. At a second and higher level, generativity may equally be expressed through promoting the survival of values one holds essential to one's identity, as in the transmission of tradition and in traditional education. The highest level of generativity consists of creative endeavor leading to adaptive change in the organizational patterns of self and society. Only by cultivating generativity in the two extended forms, characterized by sustaining and transmitting self values or by creating concepts that lead to new values, can sexual generativity be modified in a way compatible with a decline in the birthrate. Thus biological visible creativity must be replaced in terms of less tangible forms of creativity.

Though attainment of a lowered birthrate may retard the growth of world population or culminate in a slow decline, it offers no assurance of future stability unless coupled with a studied effort to promote the third level of generativity. This generativity can prove successful only in the presence of a willingness to adjust to the new values it will foster.

Population Density and Individual Reproduction

The views of the ethologist Konrad Lorenz on aggression,[5] although speculative, may elucidate the interplay of several forces—aggression, creativity, and value conflicts. When man lived in small closed social groups and possessed only crude weapons of hand-to-hand combat, crowding or encroachment of one group upon a neighboring group precipitated mutual aggression. Each group served the role of outgroup for the other, and defense related directly to tangibles—physical objects, people, or living space. As evolving social cohesion led to larger aggregations of humanity, the individual members of which knew most of their associates less well or not at all, the threat of social or physical encroachment was displaced and came to be exchanged for a threat to behavioral norms, traditions, or values. Yet the individual's involvement retained the primitive characteristics of the prehistoric tribe almost at a prehuman level. If Lorenz's inference is valid, the shiver running down the back and limbs that "makes the hair stand on end" is the same feeling primates felt as they experienced the exhilaration of challenge, rising to full height with elbows outward and chin up in a bluffing stance, upon perception of a tangible threat. This exhilaration becomes what Lorenz terms "militant enthusiasm" when many members of a group simultaneously gratify innate aggressive drives. By implication, any threat, any set of strange objects, altered circumstances, or divergent set of values may act as the releaser of militant enthusiasm. Analogies of international wars and ghetto rumbles easily suggest themselves, blocking as they do opportunity for higher-level generativity. However, such interpolations between animal and human behavior are always speculative.

Population density is not the only threat facing man should wanton reproduction continue indefinitely. Areas of high population density—the inner cities—are also areas of the highest prevalence of disease (including mental illness), crime, and violence. Poverty, the unsatisfactory conditions of life in slums, and a relative lack of opportunity often accompanied by deficient education are also potent determinants of behavior. In many European cities there is greater density of people in middle-class neighborhoods than there is in some slums, so that the indicators of illness and maladjustment correlate more with factors of social class than with density of the population.[6]

A controlled mouse universe. Studies on mouse populations yield insight into population problems.[7] Four pairs of mice were introduced into an environment in which many of the factors customarily inhibiting population growth were greatly ameliorated or eliminated entirely. No predator existed, and epidemic-producing diseases were excluded. Food, water, and shelter were provided in excess of that requisite to sustain a population of 3,000. The opportunity for emigration was precluded. Thus all the major factors of hunger, predation, disease, inclement weather, shortage of resources, and migration, which in the natural state require a reproductive rate sufficient to compensate for the numerical losses they occasion, were rendered essentially inoperative. As a consequence of this sharp curtailment of normal mortality, the original population enjoyed several successive doublings, with a doubling time of about 55 days, until it stood at 620 individuals. At that point a change in reproduction took place and the population doubling time increased threefold until community population reached 2,200.

Then another dramatic shift occurred. Production of viable young ceased with a gradually diminishing capacity to conceive, until the normal age-associated mortality eventually reduced the population to 300 postmenopausal members. This was the situation two years after the beginning of the die-off phase, indicating that the population will become extinct.

A population can be viewed as a system which fabricates living products, develops them, and finally makes some disposition of them. A mouse population living under natural ecological conditions produces a number of additional mice sufficient to satisfy the nutritional needs of both microscopic and macroscopic predators. Most populations comprise those individuals forced to wander away for lack of opportunity to incorporate themselves into the traditional system of relationships among that portion of the population residing in a habitat of favorable density. A certain number of young individuals find the opportunity for incorporation in replacement of those lost to the system through aging or predation.

Information packed into sets of genes forms another category of population products. Natural selection determines which of these information products will be developed, that is to say, will be incorporated within the gene pool of the species. Over the long run, the balance between product fabrication and product disposal permits species survival with adaptive evolution.

The experimental study of a mouse population under discussion may be examined in this perspective. Elimination of most normal avenues for product disposal culminated in a dramatic imbalance between product fabrication and product disposal. This imbalance overtaxed the capacity of the system to develop its products further and to incorporate them into functional social units. In fact, the very favorable early development of these excess products provided them with the potentiality for incorporation into an adequately functioning society, but at this stage the adults boycotted the immature.

Blocking the striving of the young for participation in the basic relationships necessary for species survival inhibited their energies, except for periodic expression in violent outbursts of maladaptive aggression directed toward their peers. This violence represented the initial symptom of an imbalance between product fabrication and product disposal.

As this imbalance became more accentuated, attempts by the producers to reverse it actually led to a dissolution of their former adaptive capacities for reproduction and for guiding the development of their living products. This terminal failure consisted of an incapacity to engage in and complete those complex repertoires requisite for species survival. Interrelated repertoires of courtship, territorial defense, and maternal performance form the most complex set of behavior for this species. The demise of this population through progressive imbalance between product fabrication and product disposal was marked initially by violence, which replaced more complex behaviors required for species survival.

A Psychoecological Perspective

Examining the present human population crisis from the perspective of product fabrication, development, and disposal may be useful in constructing a rational approach to its resolution. For the past 40,000 to 50,000 years man has been able to fabricate two kinds of products with equal facility and in equal amounts: biochemical information in the form of genes assembled into new individuals, and intellectual information assembled into new ideas or concepts. These two products have interacted to increase the reproductive rate of both, so that the human population and the pool of conceptual information developed have expanded in such a way as to require half as much time for each successive doubling as that required by the doubling which preceded it. This acceleration has multiplied the increase a thousandfold over the past 50 millennia. The increase in the product that is man has resulted in an imbalance in the ratio of production (birth) to disposal (death) in existence for hundreds of thousands of years. Extraspecies disposal (by predation and disease) or intraspecies disposal (by homicide and war) has never had more than a temporary retarding impact on the ascendancy of births and survivals over deaths.

From mice to men. The above formulation would indicate that only a marked reduction in biological generativity is compatible with enhancing and fulfilling human potentialities. To the extent that the two shifts in fabrication and development of human products fail to take place, mankind will be putting itself in a position similar to that of the mice in the study described. Violence could continue to escalate, followed by increasing alienation of the individual from the group characterized by an inability on the part of the individual to become involved in any complex behavior, particularly of an intellectual nature. Yet these are the behaviors requisite for the survival and continued evolution of the species. In this context the worldwide university unrest of recent years could be viewed as a symptom of excess biological reproduction, an excess of those most capable of becoming involved in the generation and development (utilization) of new concepts. But the adult segment of society, traditionally and socially well-integrated, tends to reject much of youth as well as new concepts and values. So far, any strengthening of the third level of generativity (the capacity to change basic social patterns) to balance the drive to fulfill the first level of generativity (biological reproduction) has lagged behind the shortened interval from concept creation to concept application characteristic of an advanced material technology. There is thus a dual population crisis: as the population increases, there is a decrease in man's ability to become involved in ideas—including the idea of fertility reduction as an imperative to survival.

The Compassionate Revolution

If mankind is to be successful in coping with the population crisis, a revolution in his conceptual framework is necessary —a compassionate revolution,[8] which should form the bridge between two epochs of evolution. The first epoch, the past 50,000 years of cultural evolution, initiated a continuously enlarging world population that accompanied the transformation of man as a biological entity to man become human. The second epoch must initiate a declining world population that will permit a continued expansion of individual potentiality. Compassion, as Erikson has defined it, is a component of responsible mutuality which furthers the cultivation and realization of human potential of and by others.[9] Such other-centered action implies tolerance and a capacity to participate in the resolution of identity crises encountered by individuals, institutions, and societies. The desirability of attaining such universal compassion from the mental health standpoint, as well as from that of ecological necessity, cannot be over-emphasized. Fertility management and population stability are both "fallout" products of creative compassion and are essential to its attainment.

five | # IMPEDIMENTS TO POPULATION STABILITY AND TO LIMITING FAMILY SIZE

The determination of family size and population stability involves interrelated psychological, instrumental, and extra-familial resources and forces. While the psychological and instrumental factors are open to conscious and explicit consideration by parents, the social factors involved are more difficult to formulate and are not precisely understood. As indicated in the Introduction, population stability has been achieved in various nations, mostly without prescription by governmental or social leadership. Such prescriptions have been employed more blatantly, although not with startling effect, in those nations where increased manpower was desired by the leadership, notably in Germany and Italy in modern times. Designs to increase population have in no way matched the magnitude of population increases, which in some areas are apparently the result of death control and in others (such as India, parts of Africa, and South America) are the result of ignorance and impoverished living modes wherein sexual activity and the enjoyment of children are the only gratifications available.

Religious influences, though potent, do not seem to be decisive in the presence of educational influences and alternative opportunities for gratification. In the United States, for instance, family size correlates more significantly with socioeconomic class than with denominational adherence, although it must be noted that no simple correlations are 100 percent valid over time. The significant correlation between poverty and undereducation, probably combined with restricted opportunities for gratification, has been pointed up as most importantly related to extant family size (albeit not the desired family size, which is usually smaller than that attained).[1]

This gap between the desired number of children and the usually larger number people have presents an important opportunity for educational and remedial health service action; it is also an indictment of the deficient education and health service delivery currently available in the United States. However, information and education will not do enough. High dropout rates from family planning clinics in the first two months indicate that birth control advice and prescriptions do not suffice to motivate people for the long-term task of keeping a small family small.

Psychosocial Impediments

It has been shown that birth control is inefficiently practiced regardless of method.[2] A study begun in Indianapolis before World War II [3] showed that only 6 percent of the families studied were composed of children who were all planned in respect to number and spacing. These and other studies have shown that a major determinant of large family size is more often incompetence in contraception than any desire for a large family or lack of birth control information per se. As late as 1960, two-thirds of firstborns were children whose parents had not used any method of family planning. It has been estimated that over 30 percent of the children born in 1970 continued to be the product of pregnancies unwanted by at least one parent—this was 10 years after oral contraceptives became widely available.[4]

There is currently a trend toward more effective application of contraceptives and toward greater freedom to abort unwanted pregnancies. There is also a greater consciousness of the responsibilities and tasks of family formation and greater social recognition of the undesirability of adding to overpopulation in a careless or unintended way. However, social pressures in this direction can also endanger individual rights. Nevertheless, at the present time it seems more important to close the gap between what people, women in particular, want and what actually happens. Meeting the tremendous need for abortion already demonstrated would go far to bridge this gap, because with proper contraceptive practice it is possible to prevent over 95 percent of unwanted pregnancies (close to 99 percent with oral contraceptives). Clearly, sex and family life education must go beyond the joys of parenthood and family life to some realistic preparation for contraception and the inculcation of a sense of social responsibility in parents.

Parenthood is the most vital task any individual can perform for any society, yet it is often assumed that everybody knows how to be a parent without having to learn anything about parenthood. Licenses are required for marriage and for driving a car. Parenthood is not so licensed: Teenagers often are not even told that pregnancy is unwholesome for them and their children, nor are they helped to avoid pregnancy or to abort it when indicated. But the biological drives for sexual activity and maternity are at their peak in the age bracket for which parenthood is a handicap. People are still hesitant to provide teenagers with contraceptives on the ground that it might abet promiscuity and immoral behavior. On the contrary, requests for contraceptives should be looked upon as an opportunity to discuss young peoples' relationships, to consider with them whether sexual consummation really suits their needs and wants. People in the health professions, especially college physicians and others concerned with youth, must appreciate that promiscuity is not the result of prescribing contraceptives but is part of a personality pattern that will operate with or without protection against pregnancy.

Unplanned pregnancies occur even among couples with a high degree of personal and social maturity and with access to contraceptive information. Even since the improvement of contraceptives to nearly 100 percent effectiveness it has been discovered that even those who consciously decide to practice contraception fail to do so to a significant degree. The reasons for this are unconscious and irrational forces within the partners and conflicts between the partners arising out of these forces. Apart from parenthood, fertility itself has great self-expressive and ego-supportive values. Having a child may be important in providing one with a sense of immortality. Although the human lifespan has increased, the rapidity of change in living conditions, social institutions, and morals has enhanced the sense of the impermanency of life. This may be reflected in the considerable decrease in average age at which women have their first child: In 1850 in Western Europe it was 28; in the United States in 1963 it was 18.[5] There is an urge to find out everything in a hurry, including whether or not one is fertile. Aside from the fact that emotional vicissitudes have always been channeled readily into sexual behavior —or misbehavior as defined by a particular culture—intergenerational conflict seems to have been intensified by the decreasing chronological distance between generations. The rising incidence in out-of-wedlock conception among white high school students may be seen as one expression of these feelings.

The significant incidence of contraceptive failure among married couples despite their professed desire not to add children to their families has been particularly disappointing to obstetricians. Physicians in general believed that an intelligent woman with access to an almost ideal contraceptive such as the pill or the loop would be grateful to be relieved of the fear of pregnancy. But failures occur, whether based on inefficient application of the method or on the development of side effects which are not tolerable to the user.

In considering the complexity of the total situation, it becomes clear first of all that motivation not to enlarge the family cannot be equated with motivation not to become pregnant. Nongenerative sexual activity is simply a new experience for many partners, who for whatever reasons—religious, cultural, economic, personal, or interpersonal—have never considered coitus as something apart from reproduction. They may have connected the two fearfully or expectantly as the case might be, but either way, severing sex and fertility represents an incisive change for many partners and for their relationship.

The fear of another pregnancy may have been used by either partner as a shield against recognizing his or her negative attitude toward sex or the fact that sexual activity for one or the other or both of them has never been pleasurable. The fact of the wife's pregnancy may have given some husbands culturally accepted license to seek another sexual partner for the duration, while women who have conflicts about intercourse may have welcomed nine months of abstinence.

The shift from a contraceptive directly connected with the act of intercourse, where decision to interfere with fertility has to be made on the spot, to an agent imposing prolonged though temporary infertility causes unexpected difficulties. The decision-making not only has been separated from the act itself but also may have been transferred from one partner to the other. Such a shift in responsibility may entail considerable alteration in other aspects of the relationship—for example, power or dominance. Some husbands fear that without the risk of pregnancy their wives may be tempted to seek or may more easily become participants in extramarital affairs. "Taking a chance" may also have been an enjoyable element in sexual intercourse between the partners.

There may be emotional reactions against taking pills or against implanting a foreign body in one's womb. It is noteworthy that the alleged symptoms and side effects of either method are similar. In one series reported, 70 percent of women on placebo contraceptives developed "side effects." [6] Other women feel guilty about "avoiding" motherhood by preventing pregnancy, as though pregnancy and motherhood were an ever-recurring punishment or jeopardy they deserve. And those women who are best attuned to their biological womanliness may have the greatest difficulty of all.

Still other women feel that they are depriving their husband by taking away his sense of being fertile. Some husbands do feel deprived by their partners' sterile condition, and some feel that they are "wasting their semen," while at the same time they resent their lack of control over contraception. Other husbands may object to infertility because they do not feel manly unless they can impregnate their partners. Extended family members also may put pressure on some couples to have a child. [7]

Aside from feelings of guilt about interfering with pregnancy, some women truly enjoy life and feel whole only with something live inside them or with a young child to take care of. Some members of the women's liberation movement may decry such an attitude as degrading a woman to the status of "birth machine," and the issue does touch upon the overall question of women's roles in any society, but the phenomenon is well known to all workers in obstetrical or family planning clinics as the WEUP (willful exposure to unwanted pregnancy) syndrome. In any case, clear distinction must be made

75

clinically between the motivation for pregnancy and that for parenthood, in both partners.[8]

All the psychological and social consequences of interfering with fertility must be taken into consideration in any program with the objective of helping people achieve what they rationally plan. Intent aside, a close, intimate relationship between husband and wife, with open communication and cooperation for mutual sexual satisfaction, is essential to successful use of contraception. Sexual malfunction in either partner should be treated in order to keep the marital relationship healthy in the face of voluntary infertility.

Also needed are social contributions and changes that will insure significant limitation of family size. In this area, as in medicine in general, implementation in the form of educational programs based on sound principles of emotional and social health is lagging behind the levels of knowledge and understanding already reached. Yet the underlying problems are complex and cannot be solved by the distribution of formal texts and educational materials through any or even all media. Ingrained sociocultural myths—especially those concerning the differences between the sexes, whether real or supposed—must be dealt with. Society has made allowance for the prolonged relative dependency and necessarily incomplete adulthood of men striving for professional status and a career, but has not made allowance for women with like goals and potentials that takes into account their temporary physical handicap during pregnancy. Once there are children, the woman is almost invariably expected to assume the major responsibilities for parenting, not only at first (when she is obviously the one who must do it), but throughout most of the family's reproductive life.

Still operative although clearly weakening is the taboo against sexual intercourse before marriage. To this day marriages are undertaken to legitimize sexual activity, if not a pregnancy. Yet such taboos cannot be reconciled with principles of good mental health for individuals, for marriages, or for families. Avoiding sexual intercourse before marriage may be ideal, but all industrial societies must come to terms with the fact that the urge toward sexual activity is greatest during late adolescence and early adulthood. The age at which society is willing to grant adult status to the young may be delayed as much as a decade, depending on the educational goals and career expectations of the individual.

There is no evidence that sexual activity among the young as part of otherwise wholesome relationships is unhealthful in itself, although unprotected intercourse is socially undesirable and increases the risk of contracting and spreading venereal disease. In fact, before adequate contraception and effective venereal disease control were possible, it may have been realistic to make sexual activity of the young difficult or well-nigh impossible. Of course this was done at the expense of burdening sexual behavior with conflict, guilt, and at times severe overt punishment. In the 1970s none of this is realistic social guidance. Because of the large-scale postponement of full adulthood for socioeconomic reasons, society must acknowledge the emotional problems involved and the validity of informed sexual activity with consent by the young, who may have no intent or ability to form permanent alliances, let alone to accept the responsibility of family formation.

The states of adulthood and parenthood are taken to be synonymous, especially in the legal sphere. Becoming a mother at 17 or 18 carries the formal and informal implications of legal emancipation, although such early pregnancy and parenthood may bespeak the young mother's immaturity, as it may stunt her emotional growth and her progress toward full maturity. Among the many class-bound disadvantages that limit real opportunities for the poor, for minorities, and for girls in general, premature pregnancy and parenthood, whether legal or not, rank high. Together they may constitute the greatest impediment to equal opportunity in life and to the attainment of mature adulthood.

Ambivalence—Economic and Ideological

Another element, operative especially in American society, that subtly promotes large families and an infinite increase in the population is economic philosophy. Americans tend to regard growth in numbers as an essential ingredient to prosperity. Unfortunately, a society that wishes to stabilize its population must also come to grips with the need to stabilize living standards, at least in the material sense. The quality of life at the third level of creativity could be almost infinitely enhanced in a stable population.

But where lack of economic growth is proverbially equated with a declining standard of living, it is not enough to forswear limitless expansion. Society must modify the inequalities in the economic sphere because material disadvantages restrict educational opportunities and provide additional stimulus for large families among that broad sector which may view pregnancy and children as the only gratifying life experiences available to its members. From the mental health standpoint alone, the impact of economic disadvantage on reproduction is severe; it establishes an evolutionary cycle of poverty begetting poverty for the next generation through early pregnancy and parenthood, marital or extramarital. Once started, a pattern of annual reproduction may set in, resulting in an overpopulated family which lacks any of the resources essential in modern society for proper parenting and development of the young. Yet overreproduction among the poor is small compared to the overreproduction of the middle classes.

Whether they develop by design or by accident, overpopulated family units demonstrate the finiteness of family resources for educational and social development. The attitudes and policies of government reflect society's low priority in providing needed services for these children, wanted or unwanted. It has been widely recognized that in general the children of the poverty sector are underprepared even for kindergarten, and assertions have been made by experts such as the world's outstanding analyst of children, Anna Freud,[9] that enrichment programs must start in the first year of life. Despite this need almost no appropriate provisions in the form of day care centers have been organized in the United States. Even the few programs launched in the mid-sixties, primarily geared toward improved preparation for school, have been evaluated inadequately and starved financially. Only a small amount of undercare by communities and governmental agencies becomes visible as the incidence of grossly abused and neglected children and the number of inmates in mental hospitals and schools for the retarded.

If national attitudes and policies, which are always interwoven with economic considerations, bespeak a lack of concern for children, United States economic philosophy encourages child production. Tax laws make allowances for large families without limit instead of taxing them more heavily because they consume a larger share of communal supports and resources.

The economic system of a population is a complex factor in the size of a population. It is possible to cite examples of contradictory correlations in almost all known groupings. Agricultural societies, for example, tend to favor many children per family as long as they are needed for labor, yet predominantly agricultural nations like Ireland or France have had stable populations, though not necessarily small families, over long periods of time. One dampening effect on family size in other times and countries has been the operation of inheritance laws and rules of primogeniture. Although children are an economic liability in modern industrial societies, urban and suburban families until recently have opted for more than three children, whereas the poor urban and rural families have desired fewer children. But because modern industrial economics favors ever-larger and more efficient production in hope of and indeed as part of a tremendous effort toward increasing consumption, this emphasis on production growth may have influenced human production.

The type of economic system seems to have less to do with reproductive attitudes and practices than does governmental policy, especially in authoritarian societies. Some nations have been effective in controlling their population by either increasing or curbing reproduction at various times. At present, China seems to be doing the latter. In general Western governments seem to be more afraid of limiting industrial growth than of depleting resources. There are Western economists who view reproductive restraints as desirable for many reasons, especially for other parts of the world, such as India, but there seems to be no clearly supportive mandate from the economic profession for population limitation as a necessity. Modern societies with economic systems as disparate as those of Sweden, Russia, and Japan have low birthrates, but birthrates are high in South America and Egypt.

There is a connection between power concerns and the number of people in a nation or group. Nationalism and racism foster these concerns. Currently some blacks view birth control as a genocidal tool directed against their race. While economic policy and philosophy often favor ever-increasing consumption if not consumers, higher material production and production efficiency do not necessarily require equivalent larger numbers of human processors. In fact, population increase widens rather than narrows the production-consumption gap by intensifying unemployment, which in turn diminishes consumption, creating further unemployment. From the mental health standpoint, such disfranchisement of large numbers of people from socially rewarding activities poses a distinct threat. Furthermore, neither the mental health professional nor the student of the human condition can ignore such expert opinion about the finite character of world resources as that expressed by the Club of Rome.[10] Improvements in individual, family, and communal mental health cannot be expected in the face of further population increases.

At least in the United States, society gives no evidence of being prepared to commit a larger share of its resources and its wealth to the care and education of the young. If this is true of a nation of over 200 million, there is no reason to assume that an improvement will occur when the population is 300 or 400 million. Even a reduction in the disproportion between the dependent young and old on the one hand, and the productive adults on the other, cannot assure greater emphasis on nurturing and enculturating services for those who need them.

The present inadequate provisions for the dependent young and old will be improved only if there is hope for improvement in the quality of life for all citizens. This hope seems to be justified only if reproductive stability can be achieved. Even granted the attainment of such stability we cannot predict but can only recommend that our society devote a greater share of its human and material resources to the proper development of the young and to an improvement in living conditions, health care included, for all. If population stability at an average of 2.1 children per family is not achieved, human society may experience behavioral and neurochemical disturbances comparable to those observed in crowded animal colonies, whether or not material resources and supplies keep pace with numbers. It must be appreciated that after a replacement-level birthrate has been attained, crowding will intensify for another generation because of the large proportion of people of childbearing ages.

Economic ideology influences reproduction in the United States by encouraging a narrow attitude toward women, if not actual discrimination against them. During periods of economic stress, it is women (as well as the unskilled) who are the first to lose their jobs. During the great depression, for instance, it was considered almost unethical for both spouses to be gainfully employed on a full-time basis. This vague fear of nepotism is still of concern, if not spelled out as policy, in many institutions and enterprises. For the wives displaced by such pressures motherhood may prove the only rewarding alternative—not an ideal motivation for parenthood.

Furthermore, the differentials in pay scales for men and women, which customarily favor the men, have only recently come under attack and are being rectified only where the federal government exercises some leverage. Neither the economic system nor the service institutions have made appropriate allowances for the needs of women who may wish to and on the whole are expected to take time out from professional careers or employment during periods when their mothering functions are essential. For many complex reasons, some related to economic practices, democratic industrial nations have achieved the highest living standards during a period when they have forced most women into full-time mothering and housekeeping. This has diminished women's opportunities for self-development in pursuing interests and careers that may best suit them, while housework and homemaking as occupations have been devalued.

With the high value placed on single-family dwellings it is difficult to conduct a joint household in which a housekeeper or homemaker with her own children and possibly a husband lives as a family with another family for whom she works. Being a housewife and homemaker, whether for one's own family or for an "adopted" family, can be a worthwhile and creative undertaking for many women, but it is not generally so viewed, nor is it suited to the talents of all women. Some women aspiring to be mothers might be better mothers were they not frustrated by the difficulties that beset their simultaneous pursuit of part-time careers outside the home.

Reproductive behavior is subject to many complex variables, and no one measure, no overall population policy as such, can be relied upon to insure the attainment of population stabilization. What can and must be done is to educate people about the issues attendant upon further wanton reproduction. Opportunity for informed decisions without coercion must be made available. The process of disseminating the necessary information is not simple. Major governmental efforts are in order, if only as measures to improve individual and family health and mental health, and regardless of an official policy on population.

six | # SERVICES AND EDUCATION
FOR HUMANE REPRODUCTION

Services and education are two tasks operationally distinct and yet quite interwoven, since effective health care requires both instrumental and educational effort. It is a program of health services, rather than simply treatment, that is needed —preventive health services geared to the health and welfare of the individual, the family, and the community. Fragmented clinical services are always a disservice for the patient. Discontinuous health care is incompatible with the continuing need of the individual for preventive health services including family planning. Only planned and properly spaced progeny, commensurate with the resources of the family and of the society, will prevent unwanted children. The United States is just beginning to provide comprehensive preventive health services to realize these aims through prepaid health organizations or government-supported neighborhood health centers. There remains the necessity that all physicians and all mental health professionals be alert to their patients' needs

85

for the information, education, and services they may lack in achieving a stable and enjoyable family life.

Education for family life is still deficient in spelling out the functions of the family, the roles and responsibilities of the parents, and the stages of the family life cycle (as discussed in Chapter 2). Many programs on family life and sex education for schools are available, and in a few school systems some program is given in the school curriculum for each school year. Unfortunately, education of a purely informational nature is ineffective. When it comes to producing children, youngsters as well as older persons do only what comes naturally. It should be obvious by now that the signal failure of family planning clinics and family life education makes improvement of sex education programs imperative. These programs must provide opportunities for emotional growth in the educational process—for example, through the use of seminars supervised by persons with practical experience in the developmental needs of the young.

Reaching the Target Population

Ways must be found to insure each couple, married or unmarried, couple-oriented attention and education on the issues of family formation and parenthood. In part this could be done in connection with marriage licensing, and through follow-up of newlyweds during their first year by a marriage or family counselor, much as similar services are now rendered in baby care through public health nursing. The time when couples can best be helped to decide what particular form of contraception suits them is at the time of their marriage or before. They can be helped to guard against their unconscious needs to reproduce which may lead them to forgo the precautions they have consciously selected. A follow-up marital counseling service for all newlyweds would cost less than $100 million annually on a nationwide scale. (This would amount to two sessions with a counselor during the first year.) As the matter now stands, premarital medical attention in the form of blood tests and physical examinations places the burden of any preventive family advice on the medical profession.

When one considers that the law requires evidence of the applicant's ability to drive a car before issuing a driving license, it is not too farfetched that it should require some evidence of family life education and competence for parenthood before issuing a marriage license. In the absence of some such legal requirement, the moment of marriage may be late for appropriate guidance but it is better given then than not at all.

Family formation should be discussed with every newlywed couple by the physician whom they may consult premaritally, or he should arrange counseling services for them. The first pregnancy (as many as 4 out of 10 new brides may already be pregnant) often offers a further opportunity to acquaint or reacquaint the parents-to-be with the issues of family formation and family functions in the service of emotional growth during this period, as well as to provide proper prenatal and obstetrical care. It is also an opportune time to help the couple plan the number and the spacing of their children. It may soon be possible to help couples realize their sex preference for a second child, provided that it is also possible to abort without legal encumbrance should the fetus be of the unwanted sex.

As Chapter 4 pointed out, there is great resistance to providing birth control education, let alone services. Expense is a major obstacle. Although the federal government provides more family planning services than it did in the past, abortion is not yet sanctioned as an appropriate adjunctive control method.

The same services and educational opportunities should be provided for married couples and for unmarried parents or parents-to-be. Good day care centers for infants as well as for older children must be available locally if young parents are to pursue further education or gainful employment when they so desire.

The Neighborhood Health Station

Educational services, as well as full prenatal and obstetrical services, are of critical importance in the inner cities and other poverty sectors because women of low socioeconomic class suffer the highest incidences of stillbirth, prematurity, and brain-damaged children. These problems are largely preventable by appropriate health care and adequate nutrition. The services must be available at neighborhood health stations, not housed in distant medical centers. Furthermore, since family health care embraces all family members as individuals and in group, services must be open outside regular school and working hours.

One of the major conditions for making possible humane reproduction by people who are informed, are prepared to become parents, and want planned children is the unhindered availability of abortion. Abortion services should not be integrated with obstetrical services as such, but with the neighborhood health stations, which provide family-focused health care through teams of health professionals. Abortion should not be performed on demand without the health care service's providing appropriate consultation to any woman who requests an abortion and also to her spouse, if any. Such consultation should lead to the adoption of contraception and family planning. Female personnel are preferred for these consultative services.

The ideal service arrangement can be envisioned as part of the neighborhood health station, which provides all the services for primary health care as well as offering family-focused medicine, including birth control and mental health services. The station should be staffed with health professionals who can provide all the necessary medical care for illnesses not requiring hospitalization, and in addition preventive health services and health education.

Services of this kind should be made available to adolescents apart from their families if they so desire, on the premise that many such requests bespeak family conflict, which should eventually be resolved through counseling. Health stations should be an integral part of a community service network, with connections to one or more hospitals or medical centers, schools and school health services, and to specialist services such as mental health centers, nursing homes, rehabilitation centers, and the like. This type of comprehensive health program is currently advocated, especially by the federal government, in the form of health maintenance organizations and neighborhood health centers. It is by no means a novel proposal. Similar services actually existed half a century ago in some of the larger cities, but at that time were oriented primarily toward prenatal, baby, and child care.

Few such centers are currently in operation and most of those that are find themselves understaffed for what they consider their primary and more traditional functions. Aside from deficient staffing related to low budgets, professionals in these centers confront two other problems being resolved with variable success: One is the problem of teamwork among professionals from various disciplines (physicians, nurses, educators), including the newer types of health workers; the other is the problem of community participation in the direction and governance of such centers. Some promising patterns of shared consumer and professional governance have been developed in the evolvement of governing boards or councils for mental health centers serving specific catchment areas. There is educational payoff from participating on such boards or councils, whose members also must concern themselves with the education and development of health personnel in their area.[1] The traditional role of the public health nurse and that of the community social worker already require the nuclear activities and skills needed to integrate all the services available at the center and at the homesite in providing family health care for an entire catchment area.

Contraceptive Services

People throughout the world have practiced various forms of birth control. Methods have ranged from infanticide, especially of girls, to incomplete sexual acts and abstinence, with various forms of mechanical devices or postcoital applications in between. In a ninth-century treatise, the Persian physician Al Razi listed 175 methods of birth control, including abortion.[2] Only in the last dozen years or so has scientific medicinal contraception in the form of the pill become generally available. Even though it has gained wide acceptance, especially among more educated groups, the pill remains less than satisfactory from the pharmacological and epidemiological standpoints. However, the development of such coitus-independent contraceptives as the pill or the intrauterine devices has exposed certain deeply ingrained resistances and conflicts about "remote control" over fertility during any particular act of intercourse.

Health workers should be prepared to consult with individuals or couples in determining the method best suited to their needs. The staff must not only know the various methods in current use but also be aware of the psychological implications of each. No one method is as yet preferred over all others. The specifications for the ideal contraceptive are concerned with safety, effectiveness, economy, acceptability, and ease of use.[3]

Safety

> No actual or rumored hazard to health.
> No impairment of fertility, preferably improving chances of pregnancy when desired.

Effectiveness

> Less than one pregnancy per 100 woman-years of risk, given normal frequency of intercourse.
> Effective period at least one month and preferably several years from a single application. (Many IUD designs fail because of high expulsion and removal rates.) Period of effectiveness must be recognizable by a clear physiological or other sign of loss of protection.

Economy

> Very low cost in terms of both materials and labor (administering personnel).
> Minimum requirement for highly trained medical or paramedical personnel to administer or explain to the user.
> Easy and inexpensive distribution to both rural and urban dwellers.

Conditions of use

Easy to use in the absence of privacy, running water, or sanitary facilities.

Preferably not to be used at the time of intercourse.

To be used at an easily recognized and remembered time, preferably associated with menstrual period or specified days.

Implementation easily ascertainable at time of intercourse (e.g., by threads attached to IUD).

Acceptability

Minimum interference with normal sexual satisfaction.

Minimum violation of norms, taboos, or beliefs.

No undesirable side effects (nausea, discomfort, bleeding, skin discoloration, etc.).

Must be acceptable to both partners.

Applicability

Usable by women of all ages, regardless of how many children they have had.

The two most efficient methods for women seeking temporary infertility are oral contraception and the intrauterine devices (IUDs). But the need for further research to discover the ideal contraceptive and the psychological aspects of voluntary infertility persists.

The steroidal hormone pills act through pituitary suppression of ovulation and changes in sex hormone balance. Effec-

93

tiveness is about 99 percent, but so far daily dosage is required. Side effects of concern are thromboembolic complications and possible carcinogenesis. The latter risk is hypothetical to date, the former of questionable statistical significance.[4] Under medical supervision the pill can be safely self-administered and physicians can advise the user what side effects are indications for discontinuing it in favor of another type of contraception.[5]

During the first few weeks, some side effects of oral contraceptives are unpleasant. For instance, breast discomfort, headaches, and libidinal changes may be experienced, as well as depressive symptoms. Often these effects are in part psychological, especially when of prolonged duration, and this latter development should alert the doctor or nurse to the possibility of conflict about contraception.

Estrogens can be given in larger doses the morning after intercourse. Although highly effective, estrogen produces many undesirable symptoms.[6]

The mode of action of the intrauterine devices is not definitely known. The plastic IUDs are designed in the form of a loop, coil, spring, shell, spiral, bow, or ring. Side effects are dysmenorrhea (painful menstruation) and menorrhagia (excessive menstrual discharge), which seem to increase in frequency with increasing size of the device. Expulsion may be related to an irritable uterus. Patients with one expulsion have a recurrence rate of 37 percent. Endometritis (inflammation of the lining of the uterus) may be induced by the IUD and can be treated with the device in place. Depending on the technique used, uterine perforation occurs in one out of every thousand insertions. The risk of intestinal obstruction follow-ing perforation exists only in the case of the closed device.

Parents or nonparents who want permanent protection from conception can be sterilized after appropriate consultation and discussion. Surgical sterilization for both men and women seems to be gaining wider acceptance than formerly. In the United States men have been more reluctant than women to have themselves sterilized. The ratio is reputedly three women for every man. This situation seems to be changing as more men seek vasectomy. It is estimated that 3 million men in the United States have undergone this minor surgical office procedure and that 1 million of them sought the operation in 1972.[7] Sperm preservation (through freezing) is also on the increase as a kind of insurance in the event the candidate should want another child after vasectomy, which is often irreversible.

Tubal ligation of women is a hospital procedure and its popularity therefore more accurately assessable, although no statistics have been published. An outpatient procedure con-sisting of tubal cauterization through tiny openings in the abdominal wall is currently being tested.

Permanent infertility, whether voluntary or involuntary, carries the same potential for psychological and marital con-flict as does temporary infertility. In one series of vasectomy follow-ups such disturbances ran as high as 30 percent,[8] al-though no statistically valid study of a representative cohort has so far been reported. Questionnaire surveys have indicated that 9 out of 10 sterilized men or women feel satisfied with their postoperative condition.[9]

Other methods of contraception are available, but from the mental health point of view the method itself is not important except for the emotional complications and the potential psychosocial drawbacks involved. The emotional and motivational factors require exploration with each couple. The passive, compliant woman may prefer to have an IUD inserted, or might want her husband to assume contraceptive responsibility, while the woman desiring to be in control may be better off on oral contraception. Couples who have intercourse only rarely may find coitus-connected birth control most suitable. The IUD is cheap, and has the advantage of not requiring daily action. Whatever the method chosen, educational preparation for the responsibilities of parenthood and family limitation should be part of all contraceptive counseling. Yet the research for an ideal contraceptive obviously must continue.

Abortion Services

Abortion is a widely practiced form of family limitation or avoidance of offspring. It is the most commonly employed type of birth control in some Eastern European countries and in Japan, as it may be in other countries where, because the practice is contrary to law, statistics are not available. In Hungary, two out of three pregnancies are aborted. In New York City the number of abortions currently equals the total of full-term deliveries. However, in New York City only about 60 percent of recorded abortions are performed on city residents. Out-of-wedlock births in the city declined 7.5 percent for the first time in 1971.[10]

There is universal agreement that, quite apart from ethical, religious, and sociocultural concerns, abortion is inferior, from the medical standpoint, to pregnancy prevention as a mode of birth control. Nevertheless, so long as the practice of pregnancy prevention is not 100 percent effective, abortion will remain and should be available as a second-line method of family planning, aside from its function for those women whose fetuses may have been damaged by exposure to certain infections or medications.

It is not necessary to consider abortion methods in detail. Suction and dilatation-curettage, combined or each alone, are the commonest techniques. They are quite safe if performed before the thirteenth week, in most cases requiring hospital care for only a few hours. Second-trimester pregnancies are more difficult to terminate, but can be terminated safely in conjunction with at least 24 hours of hospital care. Prostaglandins, currently under investigation, hold promise for simple nonsurgical abortion.[11]

Possible long-range adverse effects of abortion are not well known at this time except for those occurring after infectious complications. Immediate side effects of surgical abortion vary greatly in different series.[12] During the first year in which abortion became readily available in New York City the complication rate was less than 1 percent for all abortions and less than .5 percent for those performed before the thirteenth week of pregnancy. There were 8 deaths in 168,000 legal abortions.[13] This record points up the importance of early intervention. It follows that the medical decision-making process should be sufficiently expeditious so as not to expose a woman to the higher risks of a second-trimester procedure.[14]

The traditional religious, cultural, and legal interdictions against abortion, including the concept that the fetus is being murdered, often make it difficult and psychologically traumatic for women to seek and obtain abortion in many parts of the world. Yet major psychiatric complications due to abortion are virtually unknown. It should be noted that regrets expressed about an operation such as abortion must not be misinterpreted as psychiatric sequelae.[15] Despite this good record, until quite recently in most of the United States, 90 percent or more of medically approved abortions were performed for "psychiatric indications" whenever formal medical certification of need was required by law. Usually the required indication of need consists of a predictive judgment by a psychiatric consultant that self-destructive behavior or a suicidal depression is likely to occur if the pregnancy is not aborted as requested.[16] There is evidence, however, that from the mental health standpoint women who were refused abortions they requested fared less well than those who obtained an abortion, and that their offspring also suffered.[17]

Abortion should be performed by qualified professionals working as a team. It should not become a major activity for obstetricians or midwives, whose main motivation and interest are concerned with bringing forth life. In England, for instance, some centers accept the spirit of the 1967 abortion law and operate accordingly, but they find themselves doing abortions also for women from areas where implementation of the law is being resisted.[18] An efficient abortion service responsive to need should operate as far as possible on an outpatient basis and should prevent any unnecessary delay without forgoing appropriate consultation and operative safeguards. The service could best function as an arm of the integrated neighborhood health service already discussed rather than in a traditional hospital department. Besides, every abortion presents a clear indication of need for contraceptive advice and consultation, and must be viewed as an opportunity for preventive education.

Since the time of Hippocrates or earlier, induced abortion has correctly been considered as endangering a woman's life, and for that reason also viewed as criminal. This consideration remained a realistic one until infection could be controlled or prevented—that is, until the mid-nineteenth century. Although many antiabortion laws were drafted before that time, religious and social interdictions were not spelled out until the doctrine of papal infallibility was defined by Pius IX (pope 1846–78) or, in the United States, until the era of social crusader Joseph Comstock (1844–1915). Until early in the twentieth century, frequent pregnancy was desirable in the married state because of high infant mortality. Today neither danger of infection to pregnant mothers and young children nor sexual mores are what they were 75 to 150 years ago.[19]

It is clear that abortion, second choice though it may be, can be reduced as a major factor in family limitation only when pregnancy preventives are made universally and readily available to all couples intent on avoiding the birth of a child. This requires appropriate technical education and education that will overcome persisting psychological and emotional resistances to nonreproductive sexual union through clarification of conflicting attitudes toward sex, infertility, family formation, and family size. This education must be addressed to both partners of the union.

Supportive Services

Nurseries and day care centers could well be tied in with health services but both must be readily accessible and primarily concerned with child care. Schools could be appropriate locations for day care centers, serving to introduce interested students to the care of young children. While a service of this kind can be staffed largely by volunteers or by parents spelling each other, it should always be directed by a qualified child care professional working full time. Otherwise the children might be better off at home, because it may safely be said that only a well-run agency can benefit children more than average home care. These centers should have ready access to developmental evaluations of the children they serve, over and above routine child health and development examinations. Both parents should be involved with the day care center serving them—in its establishment and in its operation.[20]

Other community services with which the health center must have some collaborative relationship are adoption services, social welfare agencies, and legal consultation.

Education

So far the United States has failed to provide full family health care, beginning with humane reproduction, which is also a significant component of preventive psychiatry. It has also failed to provide women in particular and parents in general with opportunities that can help them to lead meaningful lives in securing satisfactions other than those deriving from biological procreation. From the point of view of both mental health and ecology it is essential that men and women learn that nongenerative sexual activity is important and even primary to their welfare. Women motivated toward humane reproduction must be helped to achieve gratification in work and opportunities other than or in addition to being wives and mothers. No doubt there are women who wish little for their lives other than these two roles, but such goals are inadequate for most women. Half the adult life of a modern woman is not likely to be occupied with mothering unless it is the mothering of children other than her own, and the single role of wife preempts the energy of but few women. Furthermore women have the likelihood of spending the better part of a decade as widows at an age when they would be better off occupied in some productive occupation than in caring solely for themselves.

Education for humane reproduction should be aimed at *families*, that is to say, parents and children. Everyone must be taught the advantages of small families—from the standpoints of health, mental health, and the quality of life. All must understand that family tasks are the functioning of a system, a system based on psychosocial and economic interdependence with the larger community. The limitations of individual enterprise and resources, hence of familial independence, and the consequences of disregarding these constraints on reproduction must be made clear to everyone through every means of communication utilizing the mass media as well as institutionalized educational systems.

Sex and parenthood education programs are needed from the earliest ages, throughout the period of formal schooling. There has been a great deal of opposition to the inclusion of such programs in school curriculums. Some vocal opponents insist that these programs interfere with parental rights and prerogatives; others object to them as an unnecessary expense. Although it is true that on one level more is learned from one's parents about how to be a parent than can be learned through formal teaching, parents have been demonstrably deficient in preparing their children effectively for the sexual aspects of their lives, for the salient issues to be considered and coped with in marriage, for determining knowledgeably the size of their future family, and for acquiring the information needed to implement family planning.

The content of each school program must be appropriate to the age of the pupil and geared to his specific needs at that age. Young children can learn the facts of life; adolescents can learn about heterosexual relationships and how to practice humane reproduction. Only after such preparation can parenthood be discussed as a responsibility rather than a "right."

Nonreproductive creativity is easy for the child in latency, but it is not being cultivated sufficiently from then on, through school and community efforts for young and older adults in the form of avocational and adult education. Full maturation to a level of nonbiological generativity may be foreclosed by the adolescent's choice of the easier biological route to a legally sanctioned "maturity" through pregnancy. The more difficult-to-achieve maturity of nonreproductive creativity and compassion must be fostered by education.

The topics to be covered and some of the pedagogical modes for such a school program must be spelled out. Implementation will depend in large measure on public education. The full use of services will depend on acceptance and understanding of the program and on the ability of those executing it to dispel the fears of those who oppose it. Such fears arise from social, economic, and emotional causes and must be understood if resistance to widespread contraceptive practice is to be overcome.

The long-term view. Julian Huxley has pointed out that the human race is the only species conscious of its evolution.[21] We are also responsible for our evolution, inasmuch as we have succeeded in mastering some elements of it, specifically by postponing death. In 1970 there were 1,797,000 more births than deaths in the United States, with a birthrate of 18.2 per thousand. Since the death rate is obviously not increasing, population stabilization would entail a reduction in births to approximately one-half the rate of that for the last decade. This rate could be approached simply by preventing all unwanted births. A family can remain small only through appropriate child planning made possible through birth control. But such planning will be effective only if a couple is capable of and comfortable with nongenerative sexual activity, and will be motivated consciously and unconsciously to limit family size through contraception, abortion if necessary, or sterilization.

The national reproductive rate has been declining since 1958. It is currently 2.1 children per couple. The causes of this decline are unknown, but since it began before wide usage of the pill, it is possible that it could climb again as unpredictably and unexpectedly as it did in the forties and fifties.

Education about ecology is as essential as education about economy: A greater share of the national wealth must be spent on human services, including education, if good health, a goal related to the quality of life, is to be realized. The English economist Robert Malthus (1766–1834) predicted world famine through overpopulation. His prediction may still not seem justified in the United States and other Western nations, but our indifference is not justified on a worldwide basis, even given equitable distribution of existing food supplies. In addition, the pollution of the atmosphere by people and their waste products is clearly an urgent concern of everyone. Education about pollution is in its beginning stages; it is especially promising that young people are seriously concerned.

Goals of the Comprehensive Program

The goals of a nationally scaled comprehensive program for rational reproduction are fourfold. They are addressed to the individual and the family, and they must be sufficiently broad to apply to all groups, whatever their socioeconomic status:

1. *Support for the nuclear family.* The family as a functional organism is viable and has shown vitality over a long span of time through many vicissitudes, but, because of its isolation and other stresses, community supports are essential to its full functioning (Chapters 2 and 3).

2. *Education for parenthood.* Informed and rational parenthood is not only necessary to survival in this period of rapid technological development and overpopulation, but is essential to the humanizing processes that further the well-being of the individual, the community and the body politic (Chapters 3 and 4).

3. *School courses in family life and sex.* Parental capabilities should be recognized and nurtured, but they must also be supplemented to insure the health and development of every individual in the community, thereby reducing the incidence of genetic and environmental casualties.

4. *Population stabilization.* Enhancing the quality of life requires population stabilization. This quality is con-

tingent not only on a sufficient supply of food and other material resources available to the individual, but also on the psychosocial resources of his family and of the larger community.

The educational programs required to meet these goals will be shaped by the development of appropriate information based upon simply stated basic principles. This book aims at making some of this information adaptable for distribution through existing channels of communication: (1) mass media, (2) formal education systems, (3) informal education systems, and (4) collaborative information systems, especially health services.

The educational content and pedagogic method would have to be designed especially for the group to be served, on the basis of age, sex, marital status, and socioeconomic status.

Education of the educators is critical. Not all teachers or community workers are necessarily expert educators on sex and family life. They must be selected on the basis of their motivation and competence for this undertaking. They need special training in this area, and school systems must conduct special teacher workshops for those assigned to the tasks involved.

Certain developmental landmarks in family life present opportunities for educational input by means of these educational programs:

1. School entrance at whatever age.
2. Point of choosing a vocation.

3. Decision to marry.
4. Decision for parenthood.
5. Preparation for parenthood (prenatal period).
6. Postreproductive adult life.

Medical doctors and all health professionals need special preparation in this field, because for the most part their own educational programs gave them little sex education. Medical schools are only beginning to schedule relevant courses and clinical exposure in their curriculums.[22] Clinical practice and training are usually focused on an individual (or an organ system), but in the matter of sex and family education doctors and nurses must learn to work with couples and groups.

A vast educational effort is needed to help all people accept the idea of a static population. This effort will involve the cooperation of all governments as well as of the health professions. The steady-state concept as applied to population still has to contend with important resistance deriving from the medical profession and the medical establishment, from economic philosophy, from religious objections, and from general public indifference. It is hoped that the considerations advanced in this book in behalf of individual and family welfare, community health, and preventive psychiatry will aid in overcoming some long-standing impediments to responsible, humane parenthood based on informed consent and a stable population size.

Although Malthus's prediction of world famine was based on the limitation of nutritional resources, he did recognize that reproductive behavior was amenable to "moral" influence. This was a century and a half ago. Seventy-five years ago Sigmund Freud urged mankind "to raise the responsible act of procreation to a level of voluntary and intentional behavior." [23] Today it is apparent that if education and effective care systems are not successful in limiting population growth, national governments, so long delinquent in providing leadership or resources in this field, may well dictate who are allowed to have babies and how many they may have.

seven

CONCLUSIONS AND
RECOMMENDATIONS

As overpopulation has become an increasingly alarming concern for all peoples of the world, it has highlighted the need
for control of human numbers. In a world where the number
of children is fewer and each child is planned for and wanted,
every child would be entering a welcoming family willing
to rear him to the best of its ability, and ideally entering a
compassionate community concerned with the mental health
and welfare of all its members.

Mental health and humane reproduction are significantly
interrelated and are related to the other issues discussed in
this book: the family as a functional, psychosocially essential
system; the special stresses on family performance in modern
society and the specific disadvantages for children of large
families; the interdependence of the family and social systems;
the pathogenicity (disease-producing capacity) of parental
and social rejection of children; and some of the social and

behavioral consequences of experimental overcrowding in a "healthful" environment.

The psychological and societal resistances to the proposition of humane reproduction have been discussed, with emphasis on the complexities of insuring responsible parenthood based on informed consent and planning by both partners. The motivation to match finite familial psychosocial and material resources with reproductive restraint depends on meaningful work and career opportunities for women, on appropriate community resources such as child care centers, and on consonant societal attitudes and policies. Furthermore, contraceptive competence requires not only motivation of the partners but a capacity for nongenerative sexual intimacy and mutual satisfaction.

Services for planned and restrained reproduction should be offered by neighborhood health stations providing comprehensive medical and health care for family units. Abortion as a stopgap preventive must be readily and promptly available. Research for a reliable, nonhazardous contraceptive that will be simpler and cheaper than current methods must continue.

Finally, education for humane parenthood must be based on full information geared to the age and life situations of the groups served. Health professionals and teachers must be educated to perform competently in this area. Humane reproduction would inevitably lead to population stabilization by reconciling biological drives with a compassionate and responsible psychosocial concern for the quality of all life.

REFERENCE NOTES
FOR FURTHER READING
INDEX

REFERENCE NOTES

one • INTRODUCTION

1. Commission on Population Growth and the American Future, *Population and the American Future* (New York: New American Library, Signet ed., 1972).

two • THE FAMILY AS A FUNCTIONING SYSTEM

1. U.S. Bureau of the Census, *The Two-Child Family and Population Growth: An International View* (Washington: Government Printing Office, 1971), pp. 1–38.
2. E. H. Erikson, *Insight and Responsibility* (New York: Norton, 1964); Talcott Parsons, *Social Structure and Personality* (Glencoe, Ill.: Free Press, 1964).
3. R. O. Blood, "The Husband-Wife Relationship," in Hoffman and Nye, eds., *Employed Mother in America* (New York: Random House, 1963), pp. 282–305; Stephen Polgar and Frances Rothstein, "Family Planning and Conjugal Roles in New York City Poverty Areas," *Social Science Medicine*, 4 (1970): 135–139; L. Pratt, "Conjugal Organization and

Health," *Journal of Marriage and the Family*, 34, 1 (1972):
85–94.

4. E. J. Lieberman and Ellen Peck, *Sex and Birth Control: A Guide for the Young* (New York: Crowell, 1973).

5. Philip Sarrel, "The University Hospital and the Teenage Unwed Mother," *American Journal of Public Health*, 57 (1967): 1308–1313; Group for the Advancement of Psychiatry, *The Joys and Sorrows of Parenthood* (New York: Charles Scribner's Sons, 1973).

three • FAMILY STRESSES IN
MODERN INDUSTRIAL SOCIETY

1. Mark Flapan and Helene Schoenfeld, "Procedures for Exploring Women's Childbearing Motivations, Alleviating Childbearing Conflicts and Enhancing Maternal Role Development," *American Journal of Orthopsychiatry*, 42 (1972): 389–397.

2. Commission on Population Growth, *Population and the American Future* (New York: New American Library, Signet ed., 1972).

3. U.S. Department of Health, Education, and Welfare, *Vital Statistics of the United States: 1967*, Vol. 1 (Washington: Government Printing Office, 1970).

4. George Gallup, as reported in *The New York Times*, February 4, 1973.

5. Elizabeth B. Connell and Linbania Jacobson, "Pregnancy, the Teenager and Sex Education," *American Journal of Public Health*, 61 (1971): 1840–1845.

6. S. J. Ventema, "Illegitimate Births," *Journal of Marriage and the Family*, 31 (1969): 446–450.

7. E. B. Connell, "Legal Abortion and the Hospital's Role," *Hospital Practice*, February 1972, 143–150; Royal College of Obstetricians and Gynecologists, *Unplanned Pregnancy: Report of the Working Party*, W14RG (London: The Royal College, 1972).

8. Alice Rossi, "Family Development in a Changing World," *American Journal of Psychiatry*, 128 (1972): 47–56.
9. H. Maas and R. Engler, *Children in Need of Parents* (New York: Columbia University Press, 1959).
10. Justine Wise-Polier, "The Myth That Society Is Child-Centered," letter to *The New York Times*, November 25, 1971.
11. Commission on Population Growth, *Population and the American Future.*
12. W. F. Eastman, "First Intercourse," *Sexual Behavior*, 2 (1972): 22–27; C. McChance and D. T. Hall, "Sexual Behavior and Contraceptive Practice of Unmarried Female Undergraduates at Aberdeen University," *British Medical Journal*, 2 (1972): 694–700; J. F. Kentner and Martin Zelik, "Contraception and Pregnancy Experience of Young Unmarried Women in the U.S.," *Family Planning Perspectives*, 5, 1 (1973): 21–35. See also Stephen Fleck, "Pregnancy as a Symptom of Adolescent Maladjustment," *International Journal of Social Psychiatry*, 2, 2 (1956): 118–131; and N. H. Greenberg et al., "Life Situations Associated with the Onset of Pregnancy. 1. The Role of Separation in a Group of Unmarried Pregnant Women," *Psychosomatic Medicine*, 21 (1959): 296–310.
13. Hans Lehfeldt, "Willful Exposure to Unwanted Pregnancy (WEUP)," *American Journal of Obstetrics and Gynecology*, 78 (1959): 661–665.
14. H. T. Christensen, "Children in the Family: Relationship of Number and Spacing to Marital Success," *Journal of Marriage and the Family*, 30, 2 (1968): 283–289.
15. E. J. Lieberman, "Reserving a Womb: Case for the Small Family," *American Journal of Public Health*, 60 (1970): 87–92.
16. E. J. Lieberman, "Preventive Psychiatry and Family Planning," *Journal of Marriage and the Family*, 26 (1964): 471–477.
17. Ronald Davie et al., *From Birth to Seven* (London: Longmans, in association with the National Children's Bureau, 1972).

18. Bengt Jansson, "Psychic Insufficiencies Associated with Childbearing," *Acta Psychiatrica Scandinavica*, 40 (1964, suppl. 172): 21.
19. Ian Gregory, "Selected Personal and Family Data on 400 Psychiatric Inpatients," *American Journal of Psychiatry*, 119 (1962): 397–403.
20. H. Forssman and I. Thuwe, "One Hundred and Twenty Children Born after Application for Therapeutic Abortion Refused," *Acta Psychiatrica Scandinavica*, 42 (1966): 71–88.
21. Benjamin Pasamanick and Hilde Knobloch, "Epidemiologic Studies in the Complications of Pregnancy and Birth Process," in Gerald Caplan, ed., *Prevention of Mental Disorders in Children* (New York: Basic Books, 1961), pp. 74–94.
22. David G. Gil, "Violence against Children," *Journal of Marriage and the Family*, 33, 4 (1971): 637–648.
23. Davie *et al.*, *From Birth to Seven.*
24. H. T. Christenson, "Children in the Family. Relationship of Number and Spacing to Marital Success," *Journal of Marriage and the Family*, 30, 2 (1969): 182–189.

four • POPULATION CONTROLS: TWO DISCIPLINES AGREE

1. Commission on Population Growth, *Population and the American Future* (New York: New American Library, Signet ed., 1972).
2. D. H. Meadows, D. L. Meadows, J. Randers, and W. W. Behrens III, *The Limits to Growth* (London: Earth Island, 1972).
3. Gerald Caplan, "Emotional Implications of Pregnancy and Influences on Family Relationships," in H. C. Stuart and D. G. Prugh, eds., *The Healthy Child* (Cambridge, Mass.: Harvard University Press, 1960), pp. 72–82.
4. Julian Huxley, "The Future of Man: Evolutionary Aspects," in G. Wolstenholme, ed., *Man and His Future* (Boston: Little,

Brown, 1963); E. H. Erikson, *Insight and Responsibility* (New York: Norton, 1964).

5. Konrad Lorenz, *On Aggression* (New York: Harcourt, Brace & World, 1966).

6. A. T. Day and L. H. Day, "Cross-National Comparison of Population Density," *Science*, 181, 4104 (1973): 1016–1023.

7. J. B. Calhoun, "Revolution, Tribalism and the Cheshire Cat," *Technological Forecasting and Social Change*, 4 (1973): 268–282; "Death Squared: The Explosive Growth and Demise of a Mouse Population," *Proceedings of the Royal Society of Medicine*, 66 (1973): 80–88.

8. J. B. Calhoun, "Space and the Strategy of Life," in Aristide H. Esser, ed., *Behavior and Environment, The Use of Space by Animals and Man* (New York: Peenum Press, 1971).

9. Erikson, *Insight and Responsibility*.

five • IMPEDIMENTS TO POPULATION STABILITY AND TO LIMITING FAMILY SIZE

1. Lee Rainwater, *Family Design: Marital Sexuality, Family Size and Contraception* (Chicago: Aldine, 1965).

2. C. F. Westoff, "Social and Psychological Factors Affecting Fertility: The Use, Effectiveness and Acceptability of Methods of Fertility Control," *Milbank Memorial Fund Quarterly*, 31 (1953): 291–357.

3. P. K. Whelpton and C. V. Kiser, eds., *Social and Psychological Factors Affecting Fertility*, vols. 1–5 (New York: Milbank Memorial Fund, 1955).

4. L. A. Westoff and C. F. Westoff, *From Now to Zero* (Boston: Little, Brown, 1971).

5. E. W. Burgess *et al.*, *The Family: From Institution to Companionship* (New York: American Book Co., 1963).

6. C. B. Bakker and C. R. Dightman, "Psychological Factors in Fertility Control," *Journal of Fertility and Sterility*, 15 (1964): 559–567; J. Cullberg, "Psychic Effects of Hormone

Preparations with Varied Gestagen and Constant Oestrogen Dose as Compared to Placebo," *Proceedings, Third International Congress of Psychosomatic Medicine in Obstetrics & Gynecology* (Basel: S. Karger, 1972).

7. J. H. Goldzieher, "The Incidence of Side Effects with Oral or Intrauterine Contraceptives," *American Journal of Obstetrics and Gynecology*, 102 (1968): 91–94; F. J. Kane *et al.*, "Psychoendocrine Study of Oral Contraceptive Agents," *American Journal of Psychiatry*, 127 (1970): 443–450; Ruth W. Lidz, "Emotional Factors in the Success of Contraception," *Journal of Fertility and Sterility*, 20 (1969): 761–777.

8. Hans Lehfeldt, "Willful Exposure to Unwanted Pregnancy," *American Journal of Obstretrics and Gynecology*, 78 (1959): 661–665.

9. Anna Freud, *Normality and Pathology in Childhood: An Assessment of Development* (New York: International Universities Press, 1966).

10. D. H. Meadows *et al.*, *The Limits to Growth* (London: Earth Island, 1972).

six • SERVICES AND EDUCATION
FOR HUMANE REPRODUCTION

1. Gary L. Tischler, "The Effects of Consumer Control on the Delivery of Services," *American Journal of Orthopsychiatry*, 41 (1971): 501–505.

2. R. M. Fagley, "Doctrines and Attitudes of Major Religions in Regard to Fertility," *Proceedings of the World Population Conference* (New York: United Nations, 1967), p. 81.

3. Adapted from Robert Revelle, "The Population Avalanche— People and Behavior," *Psychiatric Annals*, 1 (1971): 14–80.

4. Philip Sartwell *et al.*, "Thromboembolism and Oral Contraceptives: An Epidemiological Case-Control Study," *American Journal of Epidemiology*, 90 (1969): 365–380.

5. Christopher Tietze, "Statistical Assessment of Adverse Ex-

periences Associated with the Use of Oral Contraceptives," *Clinical Obstetrics and Gynecology*, 11 (1968): 698–715.

6. J. M. Morris and Gertrude Van Wagenen, "Estrogenic Compounds," *American Journal of Obstetrics and Gynecology*, 96 (1966): 804–815.

7. C. Holden, "Sperm Banks Multiply as Vasectomies Gain Popularity," *Science*, 176 (1972): 32.

8. F. J. Ziegler, D. A. Rodgers, and R. J. Prentiss, "Psychosocial Response to Vasectomy," *Archives of General Psychiatry*, 21 (1969): 46–54.

9. Holden, "Sperm Banks Multiply."

10. E. B. Connell, "Legal Abortion and the Hospital's Role," *Hospital Practice*, February 1972, 143–150.

11. A. Hordern, *Legal Abortion: The English Experience* (New York: Pergamon Press, 1971).

12. Christopher Tietze and Sarah Lewit, "Abortion," *Scientific American*, 220 (1969): 21–27; I. A. Stalworthy *et al.*, "Legal Abortion—A Critical Assessment," *Lancet II*, 1736 (1971): 1245–1249.

13. Connell, "Legal Abortion."

14. R. L. Kleinman, ed., *Induced Abortion*, Report of a meeting of the IPPF panel of experts on abortion held in Novi Sad, Yugoslavia, June 1971 (London: International Planned Parenthood Federation, 1972).

15. Stephen Fleck, "Some Psychiatric Aspects of Abortion," *Journal of Nervous and Mental Disease*, 151 (1970): 42–50.

16. Gerald Caplan, "The Disturbance of the Mother-Child Relationship by Unsuccessful Attempts at Abortion," *Mental Hygiene*, 38 (1954): 67–80.

17. Hordern, *Legal Abortion*.

18. Group for the Advancement of Psychiatry, *The Right to Abortion: A Psychiatric View*, Report No. 75 (New York: GAP, 1970), pp. 219–236.

19. Stephen Fleck, "A Psychiatrist's View on Abortion," in D. F. Welbert and J. D. Butler, eds., *Abortion, Society, and the Law* (Cleveland and London: Press of Case Western Reserve University, 1973).

20. Alice Rossi, "Family Development in a Changing World," *American Journal of Psychiatry*, 128 (1972): 47–56.
21. Julian Huxley, "Eugenics in Evolutionary Perspective," *Biology and Human Affairs*, 28 (1963), 4–30.
22. Harold Lief, "Sex Education of Medical Students and Doctors," *Pacific Medicine and Surgery*, 73 (1965), 52–58.
23. Sigmund Freud, "Sexuality in the Etiology of the Neuroses," in *Collected Works of Sigmund Freud* [*Gesämmelte Werke chronologisch geordnet, erster Band, Werke aus den Jahren 1892–1899*] (London: Imago Publishing Co., 1948), translated by Stephen Fleck.

FOR FURTHER READING

Ackerman, N. W. *The Psychodynamics of Family Life*. New York: Basic Books, 1958.

Badger, E. D. "A Mothers' Training Program: The Road to a Purposeful Existence," *Children*, 18(1971): 168–173.

Berelson, Bernard *et al. Family Planning and Population Programs*. Chicago: University of Chicago Press, 1966.

Bibring, Grete *et al.* "A Study of the Psychological Processes in Pregnancy and of the Earliest Mother-Child Relationship," *Psychoanalytic Study of the Child*, 16(1961): 9–24.

Blake, Judah. "Population Policy for Americans: Is the Government Being Misled?" *Science*, 164(1969): 522–528.

Bowlby, John. *Child Care and the Growth of Love*. Baltimore: Penguin Books, 1965.

Calderone, Mary S. *Manual of Contraceptive Practice*. Baltimore: Williams & Wilkins, 1964.

Callahan, Daniel. *Abortion, Law, Choice and Morality*. London: MacMillan, 1970.

Carton, Jacqueline, and Carton, John. "Evaluation of a Sex Education Program for Children and Their Parents: Attitude and Interactional Changes," *The Family Coordinator*, 20, 4(1971): 377–386.

Coles, Robert. *Children of Crisis*. Boston: Little, Brown, 1967.

Day, L. H., and Day, Alice. *Too Many Americans*. Boston: Houghton Mifflin, 1965.

Deutsch, Helen. *Psychology of Women*, Vol. 2: *Motherhood*. New York: Grune & Stratton, 1945.

Dyer, E. D. "Parenthood as Crisis: A Re-Study," *Marriage and Family Living*, 25(1963): 196–201.

Fleck, Stephen. "The Role of the Family in Psychiatry," in A. M. Friedman and H. Kaplan, eds., *Human Behavior*. New York: Atheneum, 1972, pp. 241–247.

Gebhard, P. H., *et al. Pregnancy, Birth and Abortion*. New York: Harper & Row, 1958.

Gluck, Sheldon, and Gluck, Eleanor. *Unraveling Juvenile Delinquency*. New York: The Commonwealth Fund, 1950.

Guttmacher, A. F. "The Population Problem," *Obstetrics and Gynecology*, 16(1960): 127–128.

Jenkins, R. L. "The Significance of Maternal Rejection of Pregnancy for the Future Development of the Child," in Harold Rosen, ed., *Therapeutic Abortion*. New York: Julian Press, 1954, pp. 269–275.

Kinsey, A. C. *et al. Sexual Behavior in the Human Female*. Philadelphia: W. B. Saunders, 1953.

Kuchera, L. K. "Postcoital Contraception with Diethylstilbestrol," *Journal of the American Medical Association*, 2, 4(1971): 562–563.

Lader, Lawrence. *Abortion.* New York: Bobbs-Merrill, 1966.

Lidz, Theodore. *The Family and Human Adaptation.* New York; International Universities Press, 1963.

Loudon, I. S. L. "The Importance of Training for the Family Planning Services," *Family Planning,* 18(1969): 111–115.

Luckey, E. B., and Bain, J. K. "Children: A Factor in Marital Satisfaction," *Journal of Marriage and the Family,* 32(1970): 43–44.

Mead, Margaret. *Male and Female.* New York: William Morrow, 1949.

National Academy of Sciences. *Rapid Population Growth.* Baltimore: Johns Hopkins University Press, 1971.

Osofsky, J. D., and Osofsky, H. J. "The Psychological Reactions of Patients to Legalized Abortion," *American Journal of Orthopsychiatry,* 42(1972): 48–60.

Pierson, E. C. *Sex Is Never an Emergency.* Philadelphia: Lippincott, 1971.

Pohlman, Erik. *The Psychology of Birth Planning.* Cambridge, Mass.: Schenkman Publishing Co., 1969.

Population Council. "Fertility Studies: Knowledge, Attitude and Practice," *Studies in Family Planning,* no. 7, 1965, pp. 1–10.

Racy, John. "Ten Misuses of Sex," *Medical Aspects of Human Sexuality,* 5(1971): 136–145.

Rock, John. *The Time Has Come.* New York: Alfred A. Knopf, 1963.

Rossi, Alice. "Equality Between the Sexes: An Immodest Proposal," *Daedalus* 93(1964): 607–652.

————. "Transition to Parenthood," *Journal of Marriage and Family Living,* 30(1968): 26–39.

Sontag, L. W. "Effect of Maternal Emotions on Fetal Development," in J. Kroger, ed., *Psychosomatic Gynecology.* North Hollywood: Wilshire Book Co., 1962, pp. 8–13.

INDEX

GAP COMMITTEES, MEMBERS, AND OFFICERS

(*as of November 1, 1973*)

COMMITTEES

ADOLESCENCE
Joseph D. Noshpitz, Washington, D.C., *Chairman*
Warren J. Gadpaille, Englewood, Colo.
Charles A. Malone, Philadelphia, Pa.
Silvio J. Onesti, Jr., Boston, Mass.
Jeanne Spurlock, Nashville, Tenn.
Sidney L. Werkman, Denver, Colo.

AGING
Robert N. Butler, Washington, D.C., *Chairman*
Charles M. Gaitz, Houston, Tex.
Alvin I. Goldfarb, New York, N.Y.
Lawrence F. Greenleigh, Los Angeles, Calif.
Maurice E. Linden, Philadelphia, Pa.
Robert D. Patterson, Lexington, Mass.
Prescott W. Thompson, San Jose, Calif.

Montague Ullman, Brooklyn, N.Y.
Jack Weinberg, Chicago, Ill.

CHILD PSYCHIATRY
Joseph M. Green, Tucson, Ariz., *Chairman*
E. James Anthony, St. Louis, Mo.
James M. Bell, Canaan, N.Y.
Harlow Donald Dunton, New York, N.Y.
John F. Kenward, Chicago, Ill.
John F. McDermott, Jr., Honolulu, Hawaii
Exie E. Welsch, New York, N.Y.
Virginia N. Wilking, New York, N.Y.

THE COLLEGE STUDENT
Robert L. Arnstein, Hamden, Conn., *Chairman*
Harrison P. Eddy, New York, N.Y.

Malkah Tolpin Notman, Brookline, Mass.
Gloria C. Onque, Pittsburgh, Pa.
Kent E. Robinson, Towson, Md.
Earle Silber, Chevy Chase, Md.
Tom G. Stauffer, White Plains, N.Y.

THE FAMILY
Joseph Satten, San Francisco, Calif., *Chairman*
C. Christian Beels, Bronx, N.Y.
Ivan Boszormenyi-Nagy, Wyncote, Pa.
Murray Bowen, Chevy Chase, Md.
Henry U. Grunebaum, Boston, Mass.
Margaret M. Lawrence, Pomona, N.Y.
Henry D. Lederer, Washington, D.C.
David Mendell, Houston, Tex.
Norman L. Paul, Cambridge, Mass.
Israel Zwerling, Bronx, N.Y.

GOVERNMENTAL AGENCIES
Paul Chodoff, Washington, D.C., *Chairman*
William S. Allerton, Richmond, Va.
Albert M. Biele, Philadelphia, Pa.
Sidney S. Goldensohn, Jamaica, N.Y.
John E. Nardini, Bethesda, Md.
Donald B. Peterson, Fulton, Mo.
Harvey L. P. Resnik, Chevy Chase, Md.
Harold Rosen, Baltimore, Md.

INTERNATIONAL RELATIONS
Bryant M. Wedge, Washington, D.C., *Chairman*
Francis F. Barnes, Chevy Chase, Md.
Eric A. Baum, Cambridge, Mass.

Eugene Brody, Baltimore, Md.
Alexander Gralnick, Port Chester, N.Y.
Rita R. Rogers, Torrance, Calif.
Bertram H. Schaffner, New York, N.Y.
Mottram P. Torre, New Orleans, La.
Roy M. Whitman, Cincinnati, Ohio
Ronald M. Wintrob, Hartford, Conn.

MEDICAL EDUCATION
Saul I. Harrison, Ann Arbor, Mich., *Chairman*
Raymond Feldman, Boulder, Colo.
David R. Hawkins, Charlottesville, Va.
Harold I. Lief, Philadelphia, Pa.
John E. Mack, Chestnut Hill, Mass.
David S. Sanders, Los Angeles, Calif.
Robert Alan Senescu, Albuquerque, N.M.
Bryce Templeton, Philadelphia, Pa.
Paul Tyler Wilson, Bethesda, Md.

MENTAL HEALTH SERVICES
W. Walter Menninger, Topeka, Kans., *Chairman*
Allan Beigel, Tucson, Ariz.
H. Keith H. Brodie, Menlo Park, Calif.
Eugene M. Caffey, Jr., Washington, D.C.
Merrill T. Eaton, Omaha, Nebr.
Archie R. Foley, New York, N.Y.
James B. Funkhouser, Richmond, Va.
Robert S. Garber, Belle Mead, N.J.
Stanley Hammons, Frankfort, Ky.
Alan I. Levenson, Tucson, Ariz.
Donald Scherl, Boston, Mass.

Perry C. Talkington, Dallas. Tex.
Jack A. Wolford, Pittsburgh, Pa.

137

Paul E. Huston, Iowa City, Iowa

Jack H. Mendelson, Boston, Mass.

Richard E. Renneker, Los Angeles, Calif.

George E. Ruff, Philadelphia, Pa.

Albert J. Silverman, Ann Arbor, Mich.

George E. Vaillant, Cambridge, Mass.

PUBLIC EDUCATION

Miles F. Shore, Boston, Mass., *Chairman*

Leo H. Bartemeier, Baltimore, Md.

Mildred Mitchell Bateman, Charleston, S.C.

Robert J. Campbell, New York, N.Y.

James A. Knight, New Orleans, La.

John P. Lambert, Katonah, N.Y.

Norman L. Loux, Sellersville, Pa.

Peter A. Martin, Southfield, Mich.

Mabel Ross, Chicago, Ill.

Julius Schreiber, Washington, D.C.

Robert H. Sharpley, Brookline, Mass.

Robert A. Solow, Beverly Hills, Calif.

Kent A. Zimmerman, Berkeley, Calif.

RESEARCH

Morris A. Lipton, Chapel Hill, N.C., *Chairman*

Stanley E. Eldred, Belmont, Mass.

Louis A. Gottschalk, Irvine, Calif.

Donald F. Klein, Glen Oaks, N.Y.

Gerald L. Klerman, Boston, Mass.

Ralph R. Notman, Brookline, Mass.

Alfred H. Stanton, Wellesley Hills, Mass.

Eberhard H. Uhlenhuth, Chicago, Ill.

SOCIAL ISSUES

Roy W. Menninger, Topeka, Kans., *Chairman*

Viola W. Bernard, New York, N.Y.

Roderic Gorney, Los Angeles, Calif.

Lester Grinspoon, Boston, Mass.

Judd Marmor, Los Angeles, Calif.

Peter B. Neubauer, New York, N.Y.

Perry Ottenberg, Merion Station, Pa.

Kendon W. Smith, Piermont, N.Y.

Raymond G. Wilkerson, Chicago, Ill.

THERAPEUTIC CARE

Robert W. Gibson, Towson, Md., *Chairman*

Bernard Bandler, Boston, Mass.

Ian L. W. Clancey, Ottawa, Canada

Thomas E. Curtis, Chapel Hill, N.C.

Harold A. Greenberg, Silver Spring, Md.

Milton Kramer, Cincinnati, Ohio

Orlando B. Lightfoot, Boston, Mass.

Melvin Sabshin, Chicago, Ill.

Robert E. Switzer, Topeka, Kans.

THERAPY

Justin Simon, Berkeley, Calif., *Chairman*

Henry W. Brosin, Tucson, Ariz.

Peter H. Knapp, Boston, Mass.

Eugene Meyer, Baltimore, Md.

Robert Michels, New York, N.Y.

William C. Offenkrantz, Chicago, Ill.

William L. Peltz, Manchester, Vt.

Franz K. Reichsman, Brooklyn, N.Y.

Lewis L. Robbins, Glen Oaks, N.Y.

Richard I. Shader, Newton Centre, Mass.

Harley C. Shands, New York, N.Y.
Herbert Weiner, Stanford, Calif.

MEMBERS

Carlos C. Alden, Jr., Buffalo, N.Y.
William H. Anderson, Springfield, Ill.
Charlotte G. Babcock, Pittsburgh, Pa.
Grace Baker, New York, N.Y.
Walter E. Barton, Washington, D.C.
Anne R. Benjamin, Chicago, Ill.
Ivan C. Berlien, Coral Gables, Fla.
Sidney Berman, Washington, D.C.
Grete L. Bibring, Cambridge, Mass.
Edward G. Billings, Denver, Colo.
Carl A. L. Binger, Cambridge, Mass.
H. Waldo Bird, St. Louis, Mo.
Wilfred Bloomberg, Boston, Mass.
Peter W. Bowman, Pownal, Maine
Matthew Brody, Brooklyn, N.Y.
Ewald W. Busse, Durham, N.H.
Dale Cameron, Geneva, Switzerland
Norman Cameron, Tucson, Ariz.
Gerald Caplan, Boston, Mass.
Hugh T. Carmichael, Washington, D.C.
Jules V. Coleman, New Haven, Conn.
Robert Coles, Cambridge, Mass.
Harvey H. Corman, New York, N.Y.
Frank J. Curran, New York, N.Y.
Robert S. Daniels, Cincinnati, Ohio
William D. Davidson, Washington, D.C.
Leonard J. Duhl, Berkeley, Calif.
Lloyd C. Elam, Nashville, Tenn.

Joel Elkes, Baltimore, Md.
Joseph T. English, New York, N.Y.
Louis C. English, Pomona, N.Y.
O. Spurgeon English, Narberth, Pa.
Jack R. Ewalt, Boston, Mass.
Dana L. Farnsworth, Boston, Mass.
Malcolm J. Farrell, Waverley, Mass.
Alfred Flarsheim, Chicago, Ill.
Alan Frank, Albuquerque, N.M.
Moses M. Frohlich, Ann Arbor, Mich.
Daniel H. Funkenstein, Boston, Mass.
Albert J. Glass, Chicago, Ill.
Milton Greenblatt, Boston, Mass.
Maurice H. Greenhill, Scarsdale, N.Y.
John H. Greist, Indianapolis, Ind.
Roy R. Grinker, Sr., Chicago, Ill.
Ernest M. Gruenberg, Poughkeepsie, N.Y.
Joel S. Handler, Evanston, Ill.
Edward O. Harper, Cleveland, Ohio
Mary O'Neill Hawkins, New York, N.Y.
J. Cotter Hirschberg, Topeka, Kans.
Edward J. Hornick, New York, N.Y.
Joseph Hughes, Philadelphia, Pa.
Portia Bell Hume, Berkeley, Calif.
Irene M. Josselyn, Phoenix, Ariz.
Jay Katz, New Haven, Conn.
Sheppard G. Kellam, Chicago, Ill.
Marion E. Kenworthy, New York, N.Y.

Ernest W. Klatte, Santa Ana, Calif.

Othilda M. Krug, Cincinnati, Ohio

Zigmond M. Lebensohn, Washington, D.C.

Robert L. Leopold, Philadelphia, Pa.

David M. Levy, New York, N.Y.

Reginald S. Lourie, Washington, D.C.

Alfred O. Ludwig, Boston, Mass.

Jeptha R. MacFarlane, Westbury, N.Y.

Sidney G. Margolin, Denver, Colo.

Helen V. McLean, Chicago, Ill.

Karl A. Menninger, Topeka, Kans.

James G. Miller, Washington, D.C.

John A. P. Millet, New York, N.Y.

Kenneth J. Munden, Memphis, Tenn.

Rudolph G. Novick, Lincolnwood, Ill.

Lucy D. Ozarin, Bethesda, Md.

Irving Philips, San Francisco, Calif.

Charles A. Pinderhughes, Boston, Mass.

Vivian Rakoff, Toronto, Canada

Eveoleen N. Rexford, Cambridge, Mass.

Milton Rosenbaum, Bronx, N.Y.

W. Donald Ross, Cincinnati, Ohio

Lester H. Rudy, Chicago, Ill.

Kurt O. Schlesinger, San Francisco, Calif.

Elvin V. Semrad, Boston, Mass.

Calvin F. Settlage, Sausalito, Calif.

Benson R. Snyder, Cambridge, Mass.

John P. Spiegel, Waltham, Mass.

Brandt F. Steele, Denver, Colo.

Eleanor A. Steele, Denver, Colo.

Rutherford B. Stevens, New York, N.Y.

Graham C. Taylor, Montreal, Canada

Lloyd J. Thompson, Chapel Hill, N.C.

Harvey J. Tompkins, New York, N.Y.

Lucia E. Tower, Chicago, Ill.

Arthur F. Valenstein, Cambridge, Mass.

Suzanne T. van Amerongen, Boston, Mass.

Harold M. Visotsky, Chicago, Ill.

Robert S. Wallerstein, San Francisco, Calif.

Andrew S. Watson, Ann Arbor, Mich.

Edward M. Weinshel, San Francisco, Calif.

Joseph B. Wheelwright, San Francisco, Calif.

Robert L. Williams, Houston, Tex.

Cecil L. Wittson, Omaha, Nebr.

David G. Wright, Providence, R.I.

Stanley F. Yolles, Stony Brook, N.Y.

Life Members

S. Spafford Ackerly, Louisville, Ky.

Kenneth E. Appel, Ardmore, Pa.

William S. Langford, New York, N.Y.

Benjamin Simon, Boston, Mass.

Francis H. Sleeper, Augusta, Maine

Life Consultant

Mrs. Ethel L. Ginsburg, New York, N.Y.